D0416900

Brainse Fhionnglaise
Finglas Library
Tel: (01) 834 4906

Sorry for Your Trouble

Withdrawn From Stock
Dublin Public Libraries

Sorry for Your Trouble

The Irish Way of Death

Ann Marie Hourihane

SANDYCOVE

an imprint of

PENGUIN BOOKS

SANDYCOVE

UK | USA | Canada | Ireland | Australia
India | New Zealand | South Africa

Sandycove is part of the Penguin Random House group of companies
whose addresses can be found at global.penguinrandomhouse.com.

First published 2021
001

Copyright © Ann Marie Hourihane, 2021

The moral right of the author has been asserted

Set in 13.5/17.75 pt Perpetua Std
Typeset by Jouve (UK), Milton Keynes
Printed and bound in Great Britain by Clays Ltd, Elcograf S.p.A.

The authorized representative in the EEA is Penguin Random House Ireland,
Morrison Chambers, 32 Nassau Street, Dublin D02 YH68

A CIP catalogue record for this book is available from the British Library

ISBN: 978—1—844—88523—7

www.greenpenguin.co.uk

MIX
Paper from
responsible sources
FSC® C018179

Penguin Random House is committed to a
sustainable future for our business, our readers
and our planet. This book is made from Forest
Stewardship Council® certified paper.

To Jennifer Brady and Keith Brady, who were
so generous at the worst of times

Contents

I

Bernie

The call comes at 4.50 in the morning. A voice I don't recognize says, 'Is that Ann Marie?' There have been a couple of changes in the last few hours, she says. The family has been called.

I lie there with the light on for about ten minutes, in a daze. Then I dress as if for a hike up a mountain. I make myself a cup of tea and bring it with me in the car. At the traffic lights in Rathmines I make a mistake, and a male motorist gives me a cross look, then a forgiving one.

At 5.17, I'm in the hospice car park, walking towards St Catherine's ward.

Bernie's son, Keith, is in the hall making phone calls: 'Michael, she's not good. A lot of changes. She's after changing a lot.'

A nurse's aide is bringing a cup of water up the corridor and into Bernie's room. It turns out to be for Mick, Bernie's husband.

Millie, the nurse who phoned, comes to meet me. We go to Bernie's room. Immediately you can feel it: something is moving.

Mick is on the far side of the bed, at Bernie's head, his arm on her pillow. Jennifer, Bernie's daughter, is on the other side, just in front of me, and Keith is next to her.

Leabharlanna Poiblí Chathair Baile Átha Cliath

Two people I don't know arrive in the room. They are Bernie's sister Mary, in a white cardigan, and Mary's husband, David. Jennifer's phone goes off with a sudden burst of loud music.

Bernie's eyes are wide open. Her breath is coming in moans, in half-articulated words. Each breath seems to be an entirely new and unknown act.

I met Bernie Brady Walsh at the beginning of her last summer. I was looking for people who were about to die and were interested in talking about it. At the end of a meeting with doctors at Our Lady's Hospice in Harold's Cross, in Dublin, one of them said that I should seek out a counsellor with whom I could discuss my own emotional reaction to what I would experience in gathering these accounts. This was good advice, which of course I did not follow.

Three patients in the hospice kindly agreed to talk to me: Eileen, Una and Bernie.

Eileen declined quickly, and decided she did not want to continue with the interviews. She wanted to be with her daughters.

Una's speech deteriorated to the point that I found it almost impossible to understand her: this was stressful for us both. She had been just about to retire from her job as a catering manager when she was diagnosed with motor neurone disease. Instead of going travelling with her husband, Phil – 'We had such plans!' – she was in the hospice for respite treatment, and was planning to travel to her homeplace in County Donegal. It is all organized, she said. We had to wait and see if we could get a house up there. A house? I asked. No, a house, said Una. A house. You know, a house. A house in Donegal? I repeated. No, a house, she said. This went on and on until Una mimed the real item: it was a hoist. A hoist in Donegal. The two of us fell back, laughing with relief.

I visited her once at her house in Dublin. We were talking, Una with difficulty, about people at the hospice. She made a great effort to say something about a woman there. I couldn't understand it. Phil did. 'Mutton dressed as lamb?' he said. Then he added, 'You're some woman.'

She was. Each time I met the elegant Una, whether she was in the bed or the wheelchair, she would be wearing a completely coordinated outfit, draped with graceful scarves. Her degeneration felt, she said, a bit like the tide going out. Every morning, she told me, she had to open her eyes with her fingers.

Una's suffering was extraordinary, but death is normal at the hospice. It is part of the routine of the place, just like the reduced prices for the food in the canteen, and the police officers who come in regularly for their lunch. Death is so normal there that you forget about it. It's like being in the waiting room at a railway station where the trains run to their own timetable. Nobody knows when the train will arrive – it might not come for days or weeks at a time. The only certainty is that it is on its way. And so a lot of time is spent explaining the train, how it might arrive, how you will feel when it does, how your relatives might feel after you have departed on it, and so on. The people who work there

3

know a lot about the train, but even they don't know when it will come. They only know how to stay calm in the face of its arrival.

There are ward rounds twice a week, and a meeting takes place in the team room before each of them. It involves doctors, junior doctors, nurses, pharmacists, occupational therapists – everybody, really.

Around the table there are more dresses and skirts and nail varnish and long hair than you'd expect in a healthcare setting. No one wears all black or even navy. Dr Lucy – she insisted that I call her by her first name, so this is how I think of her – is wearing kitten heels, and is visibly pregnant.

There are two new hospital juniors: David and Laura. Laura wears a seamed fitted dress and is very tall and thin. David is handsome in cords. He is talking to a new young pharmacist who has long fair hair and is wearing a peasant blouse.

At this meeting there is talk of some patients who have intellectual disabilities. When I first visited, there was a man here with Down's syndrome who was dying of cancer. He surrounded himself with his music tapes and a lot of chocolate, and seemed fairly content, although he did say, when Dr Lucy asked him, that his bum hurt. When I next visited, he was gone.

Another patient, Caitríona, would always distract herself when Dr Lucy tried to speak to her about what was happening. (Caitríona is a pseudonym; I'm using pseudonyms for all the patients, family members and friends discussed in the

4

team meeting and on ward rounds.) She would talk about her jewellery. She had met Prince Charles when he had visited the hospice, and had the photos to prove it.

One day she said: 'Can people die of this?'

'Some people do.'

'It's not fair.'

Caitríona died with all her family around her. As the end approached, she would open her eyes and see them there and, Dr Lucy says, 'was quite chuffed at the end that all the family were around'.

Now staff are worried about Caitríona's devoted friend, Breda, who is bereft at her loss.

All of life comes to the hospice. All the relatives and the complex dynamics between family members have to be respected, because there is no changing them now.

For example, Dr Lucy says at the team meeting, 'There is a lady in now with lung cancer – she is a carer for her father, who even by her own account is a cantankerous old man.'

Then there is Sarah, who has some cognitive impairment and has no insight into her condition. Sarah is from the country and 'a lovely family. Farming.' She has two adult daughters. They would like to take her home but they cannot look after her there. Dr Lucy says: 'We're just gauging what to say to them to make them feel less guilty.'

Another patient, Rose, was admitted months ago, in April. She is quite distressed a lot of the time. 'For the nurses, there's not much you can do for someone like that except soak it up.' The nurses nod at this.

Then there is Billy, who has just been admitted. He has

prostate cancer and developed a urinary tract infection while on holiday in the west of Ireland. On Tuesday, he went to St Luke's Hospital for radiotherapy. His daughter doesn't know whether to return to South Africa or not, or whether she can cope with such a sick father. Now Dr Lucy is saying, 'I think I might move Billy to David, because he might take instruction better from a male doctor. Billy doesn't have marrow failure yet, and they don't die until they get marrow failure or infection.'

There is another man on the ward, Tom, who has metastatic prostate cancer. Dr Lucy says, 'He's as pale as the sheets and we can't do a whole lot for him.' The nurses say that Tom's son brings him avocados in the mornings.

There are two dogs in the hospice now. Rian, the amiable but fairly useless golden retriever, has his drinking bowl in the room where the nurses take their breaks. The new dog is made of sterner stuff. He is called Spree and he is on St Gabriel's ward, where his owner, a homeless man, is dying. Spree appears to be mainly Staffordshire bull terrier, and he looks like he's smiling. He is a very good-humoured dog, but as the nurses say, he doesn't have many boundaries. This is putting it very mildly indeed. A member of staff has already agreed to give him a home when his owner dies.

We set off on the ward round. There are rooms I cannot enter, like the room where a Pakistani man is dying. One day I see a teenage boy standing outside the door of the man's room, weeping.

Or the room of the young woman who is dying of liver failure. She has a young son. She didn't stop drinking.

Or the bed of the man who used to be a garda. He tells the staff that he doesn't want to be seen by me, because journalists can be very sly.

But a lot of patients do allow me to go to their bedsides, and this is because they trust the staff, and also possibly because they're past worrying about privacy and the boundaries that used to apply. There is the lady with lung cancer, who has a shock of white hair and the astonished look of the chronically breathless. This is the carer with the cantankerous father. The morphine will help the breathlessness, says Dr Lucy.

There is Tom, the man with the metastatic prostate cancer. Everything is wonderful, he says. The nurses are wonderful. He is comfortable.

Dr Lucy leans over a man called Seamus, feeling his stomach and saying, 'You're a little bit tender.' There is strong eye contact between them. Seamus is lying back in total trust, with nothing left to defend.

Rose is angry and depressed. She has exchanged cards with her husband in celebration of their fifty-eighth year of marriage. When asked the secret of such a long marriage, she says: 'Keep quiet.'

Mary has twenty-two get-well cards on display behind her bed, and also gangrene in her foot. When asked what she is going to wear when her family takes her out tomorrow, she says: 'My bikini.'

We go to Bernie's room. I sit to one side of her, and in profile it is shocking: the thinness of her hair and of her arms. She is in her usual sleeveless top.

At the team meeting earlier, Bernie was described as being 'relatively stable' but also 'more fatigued'. The nurses noted that she was staying in bed later in the morning. She continues to bleed from her cancer, and she can see the blood in the tube that carries her urine away. It was also noted at the meeting that she has been given two blood transfusions. She is suffering from nausea – possibly because of anxiety – and there was discussion of the relative merits of the two kinds of anti-nausea drug. Dr Lucy thinks the kind that works via the brain rather than the stomach is better for Bernie.

Today Bernie is planning a trip to the Liffey Valley Shopping Centre. 'It's on one level, and they have Marks and Penneys, everything there.' She's also going to go home for a visit.

Dr Lucy says she is hoping that new medication will help Bernie with the nausea. Bernie reaches over to touch the wood veneer of the table that straddles the bed. One of the nurses quietly reaches first to the wall of the room and then to a shelf beside her, searching for some wood to touch too. (Later, Bernie will tell me she noticed the nurse touching wood for her. There is not much that she misses.)

Once the group of junior doctors and nurses are outside in the corridor, Dr Lucy explains that Bernie's legs are swollen due to lack of lymphatic drainage. She has a clot, but you don't want to give blood-thinning drugs to a person with cancer.

Did Bernie have a fracture at one time? she asks.

Yes, I say, in her hip.

I have become an expert on Bernie.

*

Bernie grew up in Percy Place, beside the Grand Canal, in south inner Dublin.

'My parents lived in a flat there for thirty-five years, before it was burned out. Numbers 7 and 9 Percy Place. Two people were hurt in the fire and another guy impaled himself on the railings. My parents couldn't go back in. They had all antique furniture.

'My parents were from Meath and Westmeath. They met in Dublin. There's eight years between my sister and myself, six years between my brother and myself. I was with my parents an awful lot. I was the baby and I went to the country with the two of them. I went to school in Haddington Road. It is a pity it's gone now – we had great crack there. The Holy Faith nuns were the nuns at the time. We had one nun who kept in touch with us after we left – we'd meet for a cup of coffee. She went on the missions and she made an awful big impression on us.

'I didn't do the Leaving. I got a Saturday job at fourteen at Craft Cleaners in Baggot Street. With Danny and Bridget Hoey. I worked there every Saturday, from 1973.

'I married in 1979 or 1980 and we rented a house in Harold's Cross. Then we moved back in with my mother. I had Jennifer, and then we went to live in Stanaway, in Kimmage.

'I never used anything, and when I was thirty-four, I discovered I was pregnant. He [i.e. her first husband] left when my Keith was ten months old. He was very good. He provided for the kids well.

'I kind of played the field after my marriage [ended]. I

went out. By the time I was finished with them, I didn't want to know them. It would have been so easy to become an alcoholic.

'I was on holiday down in Kerry and I was driving and there were cyclists all over the road and I shouted at them.' One of the cyclists was Mick, a man sixteen years her senior. 'Afterwards he said, "You were so cheeky." At the time he said, "I'll ring you." And he'd rung me twice by the time we got home.

'It had its ups and downs. When I met Mick, my daughter had got pregnant. Jennifer used to open the door to Mick and then leave him standing there. I had to say to her, "You're pregnant, you're having your own family. This is my family."'

I ask Bernie if she's always been as remarkably incisive as she appears to be now.

'I was more or less incisive always,' she says. 'I think it started when I split up with my husband. I eventually got my head around that he didn't love me. So, he doesn't love me and we can either do this the hard way or the easy. You just think: I'm not going to let anybody else walk over me. You eventually mellow down after a couple of years – your attitude. You're not on the defensive all the time. That takes about three years.

'You can't be taught. It has to be done when it happens.

'Quite decisive, I suppose I have been. If I wanted to do something I just went ahead and did it. For example, I always wanted to be working in Marks and Spencer even though I was working full-time in the dry cleaner's at the time Marks came here. I surprised myself. I went for the interview when I was working in the dry cleaner's. It was the right decision. It was good to work there. I have good friends there. I didn't even realize, girls who I wouldn't expect to have liked me, that I wouldn't have been close to, they're asking other friends how I am and if it's all right for them to visit me.'

Bernie loves these visits from her colleagues – 'the gossip and the crack'.

With her long frame and long neck, and her hair pulled back, Bernie looks graceful, like a ballet dancer at rest.

'I was five foot nine originally. I must be five foot seven or eight now. I'm eleven stone. I used to be fifteen and a half.'

She looks down at her breasts. 'They used to be a 48DD.' Her body is leaving her.

'My problem is that I have two different types of cancer,' she says. 'One in my stomach, a sarcoma, and then a gynaecological cancer, which gives me two tumours on my spine and one on my hip.'

Her first cancer arrived ten years ago.

'I was complaining of bleeding. The doctor gave me tablets, that was in Christmas week. On Stephen's Day I went to the VHI clinic, and that night I was haemorrhaging. But there was no appointment until 14 January. I didn't know anyone with cancer. Anybody in our family, it was the heart.

'I had a nine-inch tumour. I had to have six weeks of radiation. The last two to three weeks I was shattered. It had a terrible effect on the whole family. It had a bad effect on Keith.

'Then I had a sarcoma – it looks like a little wart – on my temple. I went to the Beacon. That was three years ago. We got married three years ago. The week after that, I had forty-seven stitches in my face.

'Then, last Christmas, I thought I had a hip problem. Christmas is very busy in retail. We went to Fermanagh for Christmas – it was Mick's Christmas present. And it was disquieting. I couldn't walk. On the way home, I made an appointment with the physiotherapist.

'Then I had an MRI scan – they said I had three crushed discs and sciatica.

'I went out to the hospital on the wrong day. The doctor couldn't see me. They gave me antibiotics and I went home.

'I went into kidney failure. I'd been taking Nurofen, and Difene. In the hospital they took the catheter out and I couldn't go to the toilet.

'The doctor said she'd do an MRI scan. I said, I've had an MRI scan, but she said: "We'll do our own."

'She came down to me after that, and she pulled the curtains with her and said, "Would you like to call your husband?" She said, "You've got lesions." I said, "Would you mind speaking English?" She said, "You've got tumours. You've got one on the spine. Two nodules on the lungs, one on your bladder and one on the bone on your hip."'

On the day Bernie received this diagnosis, her son Keith and her friend Caroline were in Tallaght hospital visiting her. They went, Keith recalls, 'to get a coffee and a smoke'.

When they came back to Bernie's room, Keith says, 'The

curtains round her bed were closed. The nurse told us to go off for a bit. Jennifer arrived. Mick was outside. Mick was in tears. They told us that it was cancer – stage two cancer. Mam being the way she is, she told us she'd have chemo and it would be okay.'

Keith is an enormous person – six foot two with a wide head and a big body. He is twenty-three, but his big blue eyes make him look younger.

'On the Thursday, we found out it was a lot worse. It was stage four and tumours everywhere. It still bothers me that in January and February she'd had three MRIs and they were all clear. Especially when they said she had crushed discs in her back.'

Jennifer is thirty-seven but looks much younger, and she accepts compliments on this subject calmly. 'Bernie always looked younger,' she says. 'My da is like that as well.' Jenny is big and beautiful in the way Bernie once must have been. Tall and broad with wide shoulders, white-blonde hair and luminous skin.

'You don't expect anyone to die. In two years' time we were going to have her sixtieth birthday and my fortieth – the plans we had.

'We've seen her disintegrating. We've seen her go from the woman she was . . . she's just skin and bone. My mam was always a [size] eighteen to a twenty. To see her now, she's just bone – there's nothing to her.'

Bernie spent three or four months in Tallaght hospital, a period that she and her family members remember as grim.

'I was in a room at the end of a corridor and nobody

passed by,' she tells me. 'I felt people only came in when they were giving me medicine, and I was getting depressed. It was too far to walk with crutches to the lift. You had to walk down a corridor and then down another corridor and then down another corridor to get to the lift. I couldn't get a proper wheelchair – the porters were in charge of them. Mostly it was stupid chairs like these' – she gestures to the moulded plastic chairs in her room – 'on wheels.'

Keith, too, recalls this aspect of his mother's experience in Tallaght with bitterness. 'My mam was very down and not herself. The day she came here [to the hospice] she brightened up. She has her own wheelchair. In Tallaght, to get a wheelchair was like the Christmas sale – once the wheelchairs are gone, they're gone. You come out of Tallaght, you're absolutely wrecked. Here, you come out and you're refreshed.'

Bernie remembers her doctor, Dr Higgins – whom she liked and who also works at the hospice – coming into her room one day and saying, 'I think you need a change of scenery.'

'I said, "Like where?" And he said, "The hospice." He said, "Have a think about it and I'll come back on Monday."'

The contrast between the hospital and the hospice was immediately obvious to Bernie. 'When I arrived here, after just a day, I felt so relaxed. It wasn't depressing. And this is what I'm looking at.' From her room on the ground floor, we both look out at the beautiful garden.

Dr Higgins came to visit her in the hospice, and told her that the place had given her a new lease of life. Bernie herself, ever practical, said it had given her the ability 'to get things done'.

'I couldn't be at home. At the weekend I went into the little box room at home, where I keep my jewellery and my make-up and my computer. And there was a pile of stuff on the chair. I said, "What's that doing here? These are face cloths, they should be in the bathroom."'

Nancy Mitford said that no woman can really rest at home – and Nancy Mitford had servants.

'Yes, well,' says Bernie. 'At home I would be worrying. Here I feel okay. All I have to do now is order the coffin, and I'm doing that this week. When I get this done, it's the last piece of the jigsaw.'

Bernie is sorting bills and making sure Mick has access to the bank account. She is going to write down the dates when the car insurance is due, when the property tax is due. 'It is frustrating on these stupid phones, you're holding on, it drives me potty. I just want to pick a coffin, you see. An eco coffin. I'm doing it probably so the kids don't have to do it. Everything else is done and dusted.'

On her shopping trip to Liffey Valley, Bernie says, she 'did a lot of damage. Three tops, two nighties, two bras in M&S, and a rug I got in Dunnes.'

Her friend Caroline was with her. In one of the shops, she says, 'I had a stand-up row with Caroline at the till. You know I've asked everyone to wear bright colours at the funeral – or to wear turquoise. Caroline wanted to buy me a black blouse with turquoise flowers all down the side. She said, "You'll need something to wear for the funeral." I said, "It's a closed coffin, so it doesn't make any difference. You don't have to put me in anything, as a matter of fact."

'Caroline said, "You can have my turquoise cardigan." We both had the same cardigan but I lost mine. I said, would you not wear that? And she said no, it's too big. She got me the black top with flowers down the side. Caroline knows what suits me. I've known her for forty years so we can talk about anything. I met her in Weir's, when we were both working there, and that first day we went shopping together and we've been shopping together ever since. I was looking at the wardrobe at home yesterday and thinking, "That's forty years of shopping." Mick says he doesn't envy the person who's going to have to clear it out.'

Four days later, Bernie's face and her hair are thinner than ever. There is a scab on her scalp. She is wearing earrings, and four or five of her necklaces hang over the bed. Her top is bright blue. She is feeling good today, but she has had a hard week.

'It's just the disease. You just turn a corner and your energy is different. It's like someone dragged the energy from you. I had two traumatic days. Tuesday I had the funeral parlour in. The guy who came was a biggish guy, Eric. He showed me the coffins in a brochure and I chose one. So it will cost five and a half thousand. That's with one car, flowers, the hearse and the coffin. All of that will cost five and a half thousand. I thought it was reasonable. I was expecting it to be about eight thousand euros.'

I decide this is the moment to ask Bernie's permission to stay with her body after her death, to watch it being washed.

She says, 'All right, I'll do it.'

She is tired: 'Talking about going into a little black box, it's quite heavy. Shook me a little.'

By the following Tuesday, 22 August, she is exhausted.

'I'm just zapped. All I did yesterday was stay in bed all day. The girls were washing me in bed. I could be sitting here and the next thing I go like this . . .' She nods her head to the side. 'It's all part of the Big Plan. Not my Big Plan. I'm in the downhill stretch. He's trying to say, "We're on our way out now, here's the door." I don't believe in God. I do believe there's somebody that directs you. I know I'm having a non-religious funeral and I don't practise religion. And I know it's like a contradiction, I suppose. It probably makes it easier not to think so hard about things, to think that someone else is directing.'

I ask if she is comfortable. 'I am comfortable, yeah. I have a bit of pain, under the rib.' She indicates a lower rib on her right-hand side. 'I don't know if it's the way I'm sitting. It's under the bust.

'The catheter is not working like it should be. But I've no drips. I have a pump. My little knitted bag.'

She holds up her medication pump with its knitted cover, which is in differing shades of blue.

'They showed me a selection. There was a plain white one, but I said no, it would get dirty. This is basket stitch – you knit four, purl four, for four rows. Then you go back and do the opposite – yes, it's like laying bricks. I used to knit.'

Four days later, when I look through the glass in the door of her room, I see Bernie asleep in her chair, head lolling. I go to the nurses' station at the end of the corridor. One nurse says that Bernie has been sleeping a lot. Another nurse says that she will not mind being woken.

And she does not mind.

She is wearing her grey and white top and her silver and grey necklace. She is squinting. Caroline told me that on Tuesday night, Bernie's eyes had been 'rolling in her head. She was out of it.'

Now Bernie says: 'I had to have a talk with Jennifer and Keith. This is the downward stretch now, I can feel it.'

At Bernie's request, I pull the curtain over the open window.

Her eyes are rolling back in her head. Her eyelids are too heavy. Her morphine dose must have been raised.

I say that I have met Jennifer, and what a great young woman she is.

For the first time, Bernie's head centres on her neck and her eyes become clear and focused.

Their last talk was difficult for them both.

'She said, "Mam, don't start or I'll end up crying." I said, "Yeah, so? That's all part of it."'

I praise Jennifer: how capable she is, and how busy.

'She takes everything in her stride. She just potters along with it.'

I ask about Mick: is he okay?

'Not really.'

I say that Irishmen of our generation aren't great at feelings.

'Tell me about it. Particularly the country generation.'

I say, 'What do they do to boys down there?'

A nurse she hasn't seen in a while comes into the room, gives her a hug.

'I got so comfortable the last two nights. The nurses changed my position and they put me on my side. It's great. I had been sleeping on my back. But at home I sleep on my side.'

Bernie sees someone behind me, out in the garden. It looks like a maintenance man.

She says: 'I thought it was Mick. I was thinking, "Where's he going at this time of day?"'

Her eyes roll again. She pulls herself back from oblivion by tapping a turquoise nail on the remote control for the television. *Tap, tap* goes the nail.

'Mick used to snuggle into me.'

Her eyes are still rolling. She apologizes. It is terrible to see her so overcome. I wonder if she is on too much morphine.

AMH: I'll go.

Bernie: No, no, don't go.

AMH: I'm here all day and I can come back later. Anyway, I don't have a big list of questions to get through.

Bernie: It's just a chat.

AMH: Just a chat, to touch base with you. It doesn't have to be a long session.

I stand up.

AMH: Can I touch your foot?

Bernie: Go ahead.

I squeeze her right foot, with its beautiful turquoise nails.

On the way out, I say, 'Open or closed?' which is what I always ask about the door to her room.

Bernie says, 'Closed.'

I blow her a kiss – for the first time.

At the nurses' station, I learn that I was wrong about Bernie's morphine. A young nurse with brown hair says the dose has not been increased recently, and perhaps not since she was admitted to the hospice.

Nurse: She won't let us raise it.

AMH: What is it then that has her like this?

Nurse: Fatigue. It is fatigue.

As I walk to the restaurant, I wonder if I will ever see Bernie alive again.

The following Monday, I look through the glass panel in Bernie's door. She is awake but lying as still as a rock on her side, looking towards the garden. There is a care assistant or nurse with her.

Eventually I get in. Bernie is thinner than ever.

I ask if she is comfortable and she says she has a sore bottom – bedsores: 'It stings.'

I ask what it feels like for her today.

'It's coming and going. So they kind of said that it's the start of it. The start of, I don't know what you call it, it's the start of me feeling like this. I said, "Okay. I'll just have to put up with it."'

And is it unpleasant?

'Yeah. You're kind of in and out of it. It's like being asleep and waking up and you don't know where you are.'

She is feeling the back of the seat behind her head, as though to check that it has not been swept away by the tide that is rushing over her.

'The pain wasn't there yesterday but it was the day before. They just said it was all part of it.'

Have you seen Dr Lucy?

'Her feet are swollen so she's taking a couple of weeks off.'

'I didn't think she was *that* pregnant.'

Bernie's blue eyes come together and focus – remarkable to see. 'Oh, she is! She's due in October.' (It is late August now.)

Bernie's necklaces hang from two hooks over her head, like a mobile. She reaches up to them now and brings one of them down to her: a chunky circular piece with diamanté on one side.

She is making a great effort to focus, and it feels wrong to take up any more of her energy. I say I'll call in briefly tomorrow.

At the nurses' station, a senior nurse confirms what the younger nurse told me last time: that it is not the drugs making Bernie this exhausted, but the disease working its way through her.

*

When I arrive on Friday, 1 September, I see Bernie through the little glass panel of her door, fast asleep in her chair beside her bed.

I go to check with the nurse. She checks with another nurse, and then enters Bernie's room and wakes her. Bernie says it's okay for me to come in.

The television is on. Her hair is almost gone. The necklaces still hang overhead.

Bernie: Did we arrange to meet today?

AMH: I usually come on Fridays. I did text. How are you?

Bernie: Fine. I've had, I suppose, an eventful few days.

AMH: Oh, what happened?

Bernie: Just with, with the weather and that.

AMH: What did you do?

Bernie: It was just busy. Different things.

Her eyelids are very heavy. Her head is unsteady on her neck. The motorway of tubes looks more robust than the arm that it is tunnelling into. Her poor right arm.

She is so tired. She is nodding off and her body twitches, as if falling asleep, until she starts awake again. But then her eyes are closing.

AMH: Dr Lucy is still out? Dr Higgins is your doctor now?

Bernie: Yeah.

AMH: He comes round to you every now and then?

Bernie: Yeah.

She looks at the clock behind me, over the television.

Bernie: Is it only eleven thirty? I thought it was much later.

AMH: I'll go.

Bernie: But you're not even here five minutes.

AMH: I am, Bernie, more. I'm only asking you stupid questions. You must save your energy before the hordes descend on you.

Bernie: They just gave me an injection and it knocks me out.

AMH: I'm only pestering you, asking foolish questions. We've done the important stuff before. You get some shut-eye.

As I turn to leave, I see Maureen, the wife of Bernie's brother Andy, through the glass.

AMH: They're here already.

I go to the car park and ring Jennifer. She rings me back almost at once, says they've had 'a terrible couple of days'.

Jennifer: She was in awful pain on Wednesday and they had to up her meds and that makes her sleepy. Is she in the bed?

AMH: No, in the chair.

Jennifer: She's so stubborn. On Thursday she was in the bed and she was getting up to get into the chair. She was saying, 'I'm not going to spend the whole day in bed.'

AMH: She's so determined. She's so proud of you.

Jennifer: I know. She had a talk with me and Keith on Thursday, she basically said goodbye then. We were in tears. She told us she was proud of us.

'What I'd really like to do is go to the car park, get into my car and drive away,' Bernie said to me one day. 'Not even to

23

go anywhere, just be able to drive away.' Back before she was sick, she used to drive up the mountains on her own and sit there as the rain pounded on the roof of the car.

She will not be going to the mountains again. This is the end: Millie's phone call in the middle of the night made that clear.

The door opens and a very small woman with straight brown hair enters. 'Hiya, Mammy, good to see you,' she cries. 'Now, Mammy, I nearly got done for speeding.' This is Louise, Jennifer's best friend and Bernie's proxy daughter. Everyone laughs, or at least smiles. Louise is like a sigh of relief in the room.

Bernie's head is turned to one side on the pillow. She looks as if she is in her eighties now. In fact she is fifty-eight.

It is 5.40. There is a little noise – the same little noise – on every exhale. Something like the noise my brothers used to make when they were young, imitating the sound of engines.

Between the breaths there is total stillness. Silence. So that you don't know if she'll breathe again.

The room is like a little boat of light in the darkness of other people's sleep. Keith is holding Bernie's hand, with its exquisite turquoise nails. From the side, her scalp is clearly visible now.

At 5.50, a slim blonde nurse comes in and stands at the end of the bed and looks and looks, all the time calm and smiling. She goes away again without a word.

Bernie's breathing is laboured. With each inhalation her chest heaves up and her head moves. It is work, work, work.

At 6.10, the blonde nurse comes in with another nurse, or possibly care assistant, who is also blonde but with her hair pulled back in a plait. They both stand and look. And look. The first nurse says to Bernie: 'I'm going to lower you. You look a bit uncomfortable.'

She takes the electronic control for the bed – which is just like a television remote – and Bernie starts to make the journey to the horizontal. The nurses touch her forehead, then her arms. They turn off the electric fan beside the bed and remove it, bringing a new silence.

With Bernie now lying flat, we suddenly have an old-fashioned deathbed. Her long and emaciated body is disappearing into the mattress and pillows. The light above the bed is throwing her head into brightness and shadow. She could be the subject of a portrait by Rembrandt. The light is pouring onto her bare scalp, her right ear, her forehead, her beautiful cheekbone and the side of her nose. The rest of her face is in shadow. Her mouth is still open, but now her eyes are closed. It is 6.25.

A nurse brings tea and toast for everyone. I limit myself to two slices, and then go for a walk with Millie, who shows me the room where bodies are kept before the undertaker comes. I obtain permission to be in the room for what Millie calls the final offices.

She lets me charge my phone at the empty nurses' station, and then I join the family members just outside the entrance to the palliative care unit. Bernie's best friend Caroline has arrived and is walking from her car, hand in hand with Mick. Caroline drove here on her own from Swords, on the other side of the city, though she doesn't like driving in the dark.

Both Bernie and Caroline are married to men named Michael but known as Mick. Caroline's Mick can't be here: he has an early job this morning.

Keith is rolling a cigarette as the rest of us sit and stand around in the strange grey light amidst the potted bay trees outside the entrance. We talk about Bernie and how everyone expected her to die last week, but she revived and was for a time as sharp as ever. Even yesterday, as her eyes rolled in her head from the exhaustion and she seemed to be going in and out of consciousness as she sat in her chair, she didn't miss much. I curtailed our interview after five minutes or so, thinking that she would not notice and certainly not remember.

'Yes,' says Mary. 'She told me: "She usually stays for half an hour."'

When we get back to the room, Bernie looks worse again – a shocking picture when seen from the doorway, her head turned towards us, her mouth open and a black void in the shape of an O, in the surprise of approaching death. Her eyes are now three quarters closed.

After a short time, Caroline leaves the room in tears. We are out now in the deep water.

At 7.15, Bernie's brother Andy, and his wife, Maureen, arrive from Kilkenny. Maureen takes a step back, towards the door, in shock at the terrible tableau.

Jennifer goes into the corridor to talk to Caroline. And this is where Louise, Jennifer's best friend, tiny and loud amongst the big, quiet Bradys, fearlessly takes Jennifer's place on Bernie's right-hand side.

At 7.23, the rattle begins in Bernie's chest, for about five breaths. Then there are snoring noises.

Millie comes in and examines a small monitoring device that had not been visible to me: it looks like a junction box.

At 7.35, Bernie gives a noise like a burp and appears to stop breathing.

Millie, calm and quiet, says: 'Call Mick.'

Keith says: 'Call Jennifer.'

Mick and Jennifer come back. It is 7.39 and we are all gathered around.

On the far side of the bed are Mick, who is beside Bernie at her head, Andy, Caroline, Louise and Maureen. At this side of the bed are Bernie's children, Keith and Jennifer, and also her sister, Mary.

The blonde nurse comes in and moves Bernie's books from a chair. She puts them on the seat of the wheelchair.

Another nurse comes in. The nurses are standing at the back wall. Millie is blessing herself.

The blonde nurse closes the door. It had been so quiet up to now, and it was so early in the morning, that we had had no worry about interruptions or being observed.

Jennifer starts to cry. Millie puts her arm around her and says, 'She's still here. She's just taking her last breath.'

It is 7.41 when Millie says: 'It looks like she's gone.'

Mick kisses Bernie's cheek.

Everyone else kisses her and leaves, until only Mick and Caroline are left.

Later Millie will tell me: 'I think she was waiting for the brother [Andy] to arrive. It was when he came that the change started. It was peaceful. There was no medication. It was an entirely natural death.'

The nurse with the plait is walking along the corridor now with her jacket on. It is eight o'clock – she must be finishing her shift. I walk with her to her car. She says, 'Tough job for you. Getting the call.'

I say that it was a privilege.

The nurse says, 'It is.'

I say that Bernie was an amazing woman.

The nurse agrees: she was an amazing woman. Then she says, 'Look, I'm in the past tense already.'

At 8.13, Keith is on the bench to the right of the entrance to the palliative care unit, making phone calls. 'Hiya, Paul. It's Keith . . .'

At 9.25, Sarah, a nurse's aide, and Deirdre, a nurse, go into the room to wash Bernie's body. With the deathbed vigil over, the body seems shockingly alone.

My vantage point is now different from what it was earlier in the day: I am sitting with my back to the window, as I used to do back in the days when I was talking to Bernie. Sarah is at the far side of the bed, with her back to the door, and Deirdre is on my side of the bed, with her back to me.

In the short time since her death – about one hour and forty minutes – Bernie's body has turned waxen.

Deirdre and Sarah talk to her throughout the washing.

Sarah: We're just going to give you a freshen-up.

Deirdre: We're putting on the tops and bottoms your daughter told us to.

I cannot see much – not that I really want to. My view is blocked by Deirdre. I'm not sure if the modesty of the deceased is normally so vigorously protected, but Deirdre and Sarah drape a towel over Bernie's body from time to time during the process, so that she is never naked.

One of them tells her that the water might be a little bit cold.

Sarah: The nails still looking good.

Deirdre: Going out in style.

Sarah sprays some deodorant into Bernie's armpits.

I see now that Bernie is wearing a small nappy – as she had been for a while, I imagine.

The washing begins with her face. Then they start at the other end, at her feet. The body shakes under the white towel.

Deirdre says, 'We'll take that dressing off.'

This is the dressing on Bernie's poor swollen leg. Underneath it are honey-coloured bubbles, but there is no broken skin.

Deirdre says, 'She liked to have the dressing anyway. Her skin was quite fragile, so she liked it for protection. She had the ulcer on the leg when she first came in – it oozed and oozed. Bernie, we're just going to take out the catheter now.'

Then Deirdre is rubbing moisturizer into Bernie's skin. 'That's her own Clarins one, yeah. She loved that one.'

The skin of her abdomen is perfect – unbroken, white and lovely.

Sarah says: 'We're going to turn you over towards me and give your back a little wash.'

They lift Bernie's far knee slightly and roll her towards me. Sarah is washing her bottom. 'Just go again,' says Deirdre.

This is the longest part.

'Bernie, we're just going to change your sheets for you. So, fresh sheets.'

Deirdre is making the bed with surprising speed. Bernie's head slides off the pillow and Sarah brings it back up.

A new nappy is put on with efficiency and discretion. None of us says anything.

And then Deirdre is dressing her in a black and white top.

When they roll Bernie away a final time, I see that she has a black mark on her right heel, which could be a pressure sore. Certainly she had a bedsore on her bottom in her last weeks, and the sting of it made her miserable.

Deirdre pushes Bernie's hair back from her forehead, then lifts up her whole head so that she can brush her hair.

'Now,' she says. 'Like a film star.'

She arranges Bernie's hands, which are waxy in her healthy pink ones. Bernie's eyes and mouth are still open.

Sarah says, 'Bernie? We're going to give you a little support at your neck.'

She and Deirdre bring out a flesh-coloured support and place it under Bernie's chin. I think this is to keep her lower jaw from falling down and opening the mouth. They cover the support with a blue scarf, tied up right under Bernie's chin.

Then Deirdre takes a baby wipe and tears it in half, putting half over each of Bernie's eyes. Bernie now looks like she is sunbathing in a Beckett play.

Sarah says sorry to Bernie and slips a little cotton wool over her upper teeth, inside her lip.

Deirdre is putting red chairs out for the mourners. She's turning off the hard overhead lights. She is putting a yellow rose in Bernie's hand.

Bernie's crutches, which I never saw her use, are put behind the door. The wheelchair is moved to the bathroom.

Four yellow roses stand in their individual vases. If there are no flowers in the deceased person's room, Deirdre tells me, they 'run out to the garden and get some. But the gardeners don't know that. It's a secret.'

The leather-look inflatable cushion from Bernie's chair is moved to the bathroom too, and now the shower area is crowded with the things that used to be so useful to her.

There are four candles blazing in the morning light, as well as little flat night lights.

If the deceased person has dentures, Deirdre says, they put fixative onto the plate. 'That's really important.'

They are finished now. Bernie is tidy. The room is tidy.

Sarah says: 'Normally we get the doctor now, to certify first before the family comes in, so they won't be interrupted.' She goes off to find the doctor, saying goodbye to Bernie before she leaves the room.

After a little while, she comes back and says that the doctor isn't here yet. She leaves to summon the family.

By 10.21, Mick, Jennifer, Keith and Louise are all in the room with Bernie's body. A new vigil has begun.

Susan, the undertaker, is a blonde lady in her fifties or sixties: she reminds me a bit of Bernie herself. We are in the team room, where briefing meetings are held before the twice-weekly ward rounds. Mick sits at one end of the table, Susan at the other, and Jennifer and Keith are side by side.

Susan is working her way through the death notice. Jennifer and Keith are checking phone numbers and all the different surnames Bernie had: her maiden name, Magan; her first married name, Brady, which is also Jennifer and Keith's name; and her second married name, Walsh.

Susan asks, will the death notice refer to Bernie as Mam or Mother?

Together Jennifer and Keith say, 'Mam,' and they both laugh.

Should Jennifer be referred to as Jenny or Jennifer?

'She called me Jen. Put down Jennifer,' says Jennifer.

'Yes,' says Susan approvingly. 'The mammies usually like the full names.'

Jennifer is now listing her own three children. Then Bernie's siblings.

Susan asks Mick: 'Do you have brothers and sisters?'

'No,' says Mick.

'Would there have been nieces and nephews?'

'No, we're the only kids.'

This in itself is unusual in an Irish family. It is strange to think that Bernie, although she had an older sister and brother, died without ever having been an aunt.

'So,' says Susan. 'Just round her repose here. Maybe three to six tomorrow? We can put in "Family in attendance four to six." Or you can have it twelve to six with the family in attendance from four.'

There is some talk about referring to Bernie's funeral as a celebration. 'Definitely a celebration,' says Jennifer. 'That's what she wanted.'

'And then, "Followed by cremation",' continues Susan.

'She's not being lowered,' says Jennifer. 'She didn't want that.'

Bernie was always determined that her children and grandchildren would not see her entering a grave or a furnace. She thought that would be too upsetting for them.

They agree on an email address to be put into the death notice.

Susan is saying, 'White lilies and yellow roses,' and Mick and Jennifer and Keith are nodding.

'Fourteen yellow roses? And you want them individually wrapped?'

Yes, they do.

About the donations box for the hospice, Susan says, 'Give it a shout-out so people know.'

The family want to know if the donations box will be in the mortuary chapel.

Susan says: 'If it was important to her . . .'

Jennifer says: 'It's important to all of us.'

There will be one car leaving here, Susan says. It will go past Bernie's house.

I have seen Bernie now wearing the black top with the flowers going up one side, which she and Caroline had such a fight about paying for on that last visit to Liffey Valley Shopping Centre. And the turquoise cardigan that she had bought with Caroline.

If there are no women at a death, do men take care of these things?

Susan asks, 'How's her hair?'

'Very sparse,' says Mick.

What about Bernie's glasses? Susan is asking. Would she have worn them?

The three of them laugh at this. 'All the time!'

'On her head,' says Mick.

Regarding make-up, Keith says: 'Maybe just a little bit of lippy?' Keith was close to his mother. Later he will say that Bernie grew fond of lipstick only after she had entered the hospice.

Now Susan is reading out all the ways that Bernie didn't die – of violent or unnatural causes. Does the family require a further examination? Are there any implants or pace-makers? What are the wishes regarding the disposal of the ashes for later?

Keith says: 'She wants to be buried with her mother and father.' Their grave is in Palmerstown, in west Dublin.

What about RIP.ie? asks Keith.

It will be up on the website fairly shortly, says Susan.

Jennifer says, 'She wanted to be buried as quickly as possible.'

Mick sighs. He looks different with his glasses on.

Keith is countersigning documents.

Susan is on her calculator. The funeral director's fee is €650. She is going to try to reduce some of the charges, she says. The cremation fee is €800. The flowers are €163, because they're wrapped. 'Normally there is a fee for after hours,' she says – we are here early on a Saturday morning – 'and I'm trying to avoid that.'

The undertakers will not arrive until later, so the family can be with Bernie's body until then.

'We'll step in about one thirty,' says Susan. 'We'll close the coffin then.'

In the end, the family members are able to be with Bernie until after two, and they're grateful.

On Sunday, Bernie's body is laid out in the hospice's chapel of repose from noon until late afternoon. Amongst the entries in the book of condolence is one that reads: 'Fondest and loving memories of time spent in Percy Place especially. May you enjoy eternal peace and happiness.' Later in the afternoon the room starts to fill up, around the wicker coffin that Bernie was so pleased to have chosen, and around Bernie herself, fully made up now with a slick of lipstick.

At some point a woman says to Keith, 'Your ma got a bang on the head when she had you.' Bernie had been fearsome before Keith arrived, the woman says. She used to give out to the neighbouring children for sitting on the wall of her house. That all changed when Keith arrived. Keith smiles at a story he may have heard before.

Margaret and Amina have come straight from their Sunday shift in Marks & Spencer: 'We got off early to come.' They would only see Bernie on weekends, they tell me. They would have breakfast with her. They'd admire her nails and the grandkids and talk about her getting married. Bernie worked upstairs in ladies' wear, they say. Amina works in menswear. Margaret works in homeware.

'She'd come up and help us with deliveries,' Margaret says – and then she'd spot some lovely thing she wanted for the house.

Amina says, 'I'd say, "You can't afford it, put it back."'

Now Keith is shutting the windows and he and Jennifer are blowing out the candles on the altar, in their white lantern-style holders that they brought in especially.

Maureen, Bernie's sister-in-law, sits with us, and she and Louise spend quite a long time discussing how much Andy talks. 'He was talking about an umbrella for an hour the other day and I was losing the will to live,' says Louise. Maureen laughs throughout all this teasing of her husband.

At 6.15, the lights go off.

There has been quite a lot of talk about when the coffin should leave the hospice, because it has to be brought on a final drive past Mick and Bernie's house en route to the crematorium.

At 12.10, people are waiting outside the chapel of repose.

All the men are wearing turquoise ties – even Caroline's husband.

Inside, it is time to say goodbye. Audrey, Caroline's mother, walks away from the open coffin. 'I can't cope with it,' she says later. 'I'd rather remember them as they were.'

Caroline smooths Bernie's hair.

Louise says, 'Ann Marie,' and Jennifer puts a bunch of pink flowers in a pink bag with a pink envelope into my hands: 'For you.'

Jennifer says, 'You've been great the last few days.'

My eyes fill with tears and I can't say anything.

All is quiet round the coffin. Mick occasionally says a few words to Bernie, touches her. He has to stand on his tiptoes to bend over the side of the coffin and kiss her.

Outside in the hall, Caroline is saying, 'At fifty-eight, she is still dressing me.' Her mother, Audrey, is beautifully dressed in all black with a turquoise medallion. She is a Londoner who met her husband whilst they were both working in Selfridges, and she has a professional elegance.

Jennifer is sitting on a lone chair opposite, putting cushioned insoles into the front half of her brown suede stilettos. She had an insole that filled the whole shoe, she says, but it made the shoes too tight.

Louise says that she and Jennifer watched *Minions* last night. One Minion had a camera and one was wearing scuba gear, and Keith said, 'That's Louise and Jenny on holidays.' Louise says that that is true: she is always running around the place doing things and Jennifer takes the pictures. They had a great laugh.

Eventually we set off in convoy behind the hearse and the limousine, which seems to contain an awful lot of people. I am to follow Andy and Maureen in their new jeep.

We go up the Kimmage Road, through Walkinstown, and over the bridge on the motorway to Firhouse and Knock-lyon. There are no houses bordering the roads here, only wide pavements with little hems of grass. There is no one to salute the hearse. As we turn right at the Old Bawn Shopping Centre, girls from a local school are out in their green jumpers. Lunch break. We turn off past Kiltipper Drive and we are on to Pineview Road, then past Pineview Lawn and Pineview Drive and Pineview Park. Pineview Grove is at a T-junction, and only the hearse and the limousine disappear into it, because it is a tight cul-de-sac.

I want to say that Bernie was a unique person, a great person, and that all the Pineview residents should be out here, weeping at what they've lost. But perhaps they're all at work. Bernie, who worked from the age of fourteen, would understand that.

And then the hearse and the limousine are back out again and we are off driving northwards across west Dublin towards the crematorium.

A crowd of people are waiting outside to greet the coffin. The interior of the crematorium is bright and modern, with long curved pews, which can hold ten or twelve people, on either side of a short aisle. All the pews are full and people are lining the walls and standing in the porch. Full house.

'There is such a large crowd here, it's heart-warming for

the family,' says Brian Whiteside, the humanist celebrant of the funeral. Bernie booked him herself.

There is an offertory procession of sorts, as some items of Bernie's are brought up and laid on the coffin: a fluffy toy chick, because Bernie collected them; a pendant, because she loved jewellery; a large black handbag, which must represent her love of shopping and a lifetime spent working in ladies' wear.

Brian Whiteside is saying, 'I got a phone call in the middle of July from Bernie.' He frequently received phone calls from undertakers, he says, and also from the hospice. 'But let me tell you, that's the first time I got a phone call from the person who was organizing their own funeral. Who picked up her mobile phone and called me. How brave was that?'

Bernie's colleagues are standing all around the crematorium, some of them in their Marks & Spencer uniforms with their name badges still pinned to their lapels.

'She collected little sayings that meant something to her,' says Brian, and now we have about half a dozen people on the altar, reading out funny sayings. I can't report them accurately because I was distracted by the general laughter.

Then Brian invites us all to 'Sit back, close your eyes and remember the Bernie you knew.' This proves a bit difficult, because one of Bernie's chosen songs, 'Wind Beneath My Wings', starts playing quite loudly, and a toddler begins to shout. But Bernie would not have minded that.

Andy comes to the lectern to read Bernie's letter. 'Bernadette and Louise were the only two people who knew this letter existed till yesterday,' he says.

I knew about the letter too. I knew how Bernie had wept over it, and that Louise had typed it for her. Most people have their lives summed up for them, however inexpertly, by other people at their funerals. Bernie summed up her own life, with the help of Louise, before she died.

'Hi all, I know if this is being read out I'm not here. Where do I begin? I can't say I had a bad life. I've enjoyed it when I could, through the rough and the tough, and there's a few people I would like to thank . . .'

She thanks her co-workers at Craft Cleaners, where she started at the age of fourteen. 'I grew up with them.' She thanks her M&S colleagues: 'We had great laughs and we cried when we wanted to cry too.'

She thanks her brother, Andy, and her sister, Mary. 'You've been so great coming up twice a week and three times a week to me. I know it's been very difficult to sit in hospital and respite, trying to make conversation. But you've been there for me and I know we didn't always see eye to eye but I love you both very much.'

She thanks her best friend, Caroline, and Caroline's mother, Audrey. 'Caroline, I'm going to sit on your shoulder all the time when you're shopping to tell you, "That doesn't suit you, take it off." You'll be sick of me . . . What are we like, Caroline?'

Her daughter, Jennifer: 'I'm so proud of you. Keep doing what you're doing.'

Her son, Keith: 'Please don't pretend to be strong.'

Her 'adopted daughter', Louise: 'You have been a ray of sunshine through the laughter and the tears.'

Louise did not know that this mention of her had been included in the letter, and her surprise at hearing it makes me cry more.

Her husband, Mick: 'I know I haven't always been an easy person to live with, but you were always there for me. I was proud to say "I do" three years ago. I know, Mick, you'll feel lost. I never wanted to leave you. But when your number is up there isn't anything you can do about it. I love you with all my heart.'

When Bernie thanks the staff at the hospice – 'for your kindness and looking after me so well' – there is a round of applause.

On the day of the interment of Bernie's ashes, almost four weeks after her death, there is a fire in Inchicore, and tailbacks on the road to Palmerstown.

Her ashes are already in the ground when I arrive. The grave is lined with velvet artificial turf and also with straw. The ashes are in a green plastic container, with her name and serial number – Bernie Brady Walsh 7047 – on a typed label at its neck. It is almost covered by a turquoise satin square. This final token in her favourite colour is the handkerchief that came with the tie Keith bought for the funeral. It is her family's final throw in the fight to defend Bernie's individuality, and to continue to obey her.

Bernie's remains lie alongside those of her parents, Thomas and Bridget Magan, who died within sixteen months of each other back in 1987 and 1988. A Meath man and a Westmeath woman who formed a famously happy marriage.

'If you saw one of them coming in, the other one would be right behind them,' Andy tells me.

The green container of ashes is lying on straw.

The family are going now to have coffee or a drink. I won't go with them. Their little convoy of cars turns right for Tallaght, and I turn left towards Ballyfermot, to head back to the city.

2

Big Tom

The village of Oram, County Monaghan, is very small. It has just one shop. There is no filling station – though on the day of the funeral of the country singer Tom McBride, the filling station a few miles down the road is flashing 'Farewell Big Tom' on its electronic display.

In contrast with his home village, Big Tom really was big. He was tall, he was wide, and his big head was circumscribed by a blonde fringe that seemed increasingly ill-advised as the years passed. It would be a stretch to call him handsome, but once seen, he was hard to forget.

As I approach the community centre on foot, having parked my car a significant distance outside the village, my progress is halted by the very nice men organizing the parking, who have guided a Toyota to a spot upon the pavement I am walking on. The driver of the Toyota is an attractive woman in army uniform, parking illegally, in broad daylight, at the invitation of the local authorities. She is, evidently, the President's equerry. (The President himself was here yesterday, when Big Tom was laid out in his coffin in the community centre; the Taoiseach too has sent a representative.) The boot of the car is open, revealing a lot of pristine interior. As I stomp past, one of the parking guys has produced a phone; I don't want to think that they are taking selfies with the President's pretty equerry.

Up the road to the gates of the church, a Vote No poster punctuates the turn. We're about five weeks from the abortion referendum.

The setting of the church is unusual. Past the gate, a long driveway swoops down into the little lull of a valley, with the graveyard on the steep slope on the right; there is then an ascent to the church itself, situated on the far slope. Thus the front door of the church looks almost directly at you across the valley. There is a second set of gates on the far side of the church, connecting to another road.

Arriving about half an hour before the 11 a.m. funeral Mass, I can see that the church is already vastly overflowing. It is impossible to get inside.

At 10.54, there is the sound of a piper on the road. He is followed by the hearse, long, low and empty. Then comes the coffin, carried by six men all the way from Big Tom's house, which is quite a way away. (In 2004, two men from south Armagh were charged with stealing the gates to Big Tom's house, which were decorated with guitars and the singer's name.) It is an unusually tall coffin, with a tiered lid.

The piper, who had been playing 'On Raglan Road', breaks into 'Abide with Me', which seems unlikely but must have been a favourite of Big Tom's.

There are men here with orange and white armbands, the colours of the local GAA club, Oram Sarsfields, of which Big Tom was president.

The six men who are carrying the coffin are wearing

jackets with the words 'Cairde na hEodhruim' – Friends of Oram – embroidered on them. They're coming to the church gates now.

On either side of the hearse walk the two undertakers, male on the left as you look at them, female on the right. This is, surely, the biggest gig of their lives. The young woman is in a black skirt suit with a large brooch. The young man wears a sort of sixties raincoat and black gloves, like Terence Stamp at his most murderous.

People are holding up their phones, not wanting to miss a second.

There is a change of pipers at the church gates, I think.

The women of Monaghan have fallen into two camps sartorially. It is either cocktail wear at 11 a.m. (an older woman with a trim figure is wearing a black dress with transparent panels round the knee, with an ice-blue bolero decorated with a black patent twist) or windbreakers, anoraks and quilted jackets. The stiletto heel is popular.

There is one woman holding up a sign that says 'Farewell, Big Tom, from your Fans. From the Four Roads of Glenamaddy.' It is written in white, purple and gold, but she is sporting a large black hat, of the sort a lady might wear to the races, on her streaked hair, which has been blow-dried for the occasion. She is wearing a very low neckline with a large red pendant, and a pair of sunglasses is hanging in her cleavage. She has high-heeled patent shoes, with bare ankles, and her fingernails are very long and pink.

I dive into the slipstream of the coffin. With the pipers quiet, all you can hear is the tramp of hundreds of pairs of feet and the singing of the birds. There is no wind today, or rain beating down. As we approach the main church doors, I throw myself on the mercy of a man wearing a Cairde na hEodhruim jacket. I must get into the church, I say. 'Stay with me,' he says. Sometimes you have to be a bit cheeky, says the man, who is about my height and slim, with grey hair. 'I might be like St Peter, I might deny you,' he says. This is the most action I have gotten in years.

He gets me in. Failing to find an inch of space downstairs, I make my way up to the balcony.

The altar is crowded with six or seven priests, including the famous show-business priest Father Brian D'Arcy. On the reading from the First Letter of St John, the mic goes – but that's okay.

Big Tom's two daughters, Aisling and Siobhan, are big, good-looking girls. His grandsons are big as well.

The youngest priest looks slightly Nordic, with an iron-grey buzz cut. This is Father Leo Creelman. He gives the homily. He says that the same Gospel lesson was read at the funeral of Rose, Big Tom's wife, who died in January. 'She called Tom back home to God,' says Father Creelman. Tom was the face and the voice people knew. Rose was the engine behind his success. It was a match made in heaven.

Big Tom had an amazing presence when he walked into a room or on stage, says Father Creelman. He met all his success with modesty. He was, first of all, a devoted family man.

In 2016, he received a Lifetime Achievement Award at the Irish Country Music Awards.

The locals were used to the sight of Tom on his quad bike.

That noisy exhaust never seemed to get fixed. And he would incubate chickens in the front room of the house – something that drove Rose mad.

(It may have been that Big Tom was at his most graceful in pursuit of his hobbies, which included collecting vintage tractors. 'I love them and I love the sound of them,' he once said. Certainly he never looked as happy, or as physically poised, as when he was filmed fly fishing for a television profile.)

He was a good golfer, Father Creelman says, at one time playing off a handicap of nine. (Can this be true?)

In 1963, he captained Oram Sarsfields to a junior county league and cup double. Later on, he was the first person to try waterskiing on nearby Lough Muckno. He loved John Wayne Westerns.

Tom was a keen shot, and was also very witty. On one occasion, Rose was getting dressed for a wedding rehearsal and she put on her new hat, feathers and all. Tom looked at her and said, 'It's a terror what you see when you haven't got your gun.'

Among the interesting things the priest does not say is that Big Tom's father, Sam, was a Protestant, and that Big Tom had stepbrothers and stepsisters. Or that, after emigrating to work in England and Jersey for a time, he returned to Ireland on the death of his younger brother, Willie John, who died of meningitis after a cycling accident. When he came back to Oram, he started playing bass in a band of boys from in and around Castleblayney, the nearest town of any size.

He later admitted that he took the name he gave his band,

the Mainliners, from a group he had seen in England. The Mainliners got their big break when they were invited to appear on RTÉ television's *The Showband Show* with two of the biggest country-and-Irish acts at the time, Joe Dolan and Larry Cunningham. Though not even the lead singer of the band at the time, Big Tom stole the show when he sang a song called 'Gentle Mother'. As was subsequently observed, 'Gentle Mother', released as a single in 1967, had all the ingredients for a hit Irish song: religion, tragedy and a mother. (It is not clear who wrote it.)

Outside, people are crowding around the little church; I think there must be a PA system so that they can hear the proceedings. The car parks are full of cars from all over the country, including many with Northern Ireland plates: the border is only three miles away. Up in the balcony, we are very close to the beams of the roof.

After the prayers of the faithful and the offertory gifts, a young singer in a camel wrap coat starts into the hymn 'Queen of Ireland'.

Everyone is mad for communion. A woman comes up to us on the balcony, which is very cramped. There is no hope of an orderly queue, but people somehow manage to improvise a system of dispersal, squeezing past one another patiently, supervised by a sort of church bouncer.

By the time communion is finished, about one twentieth of the crowd on the balcony have left. This is a very small percentage for a big Irish event; Big Tom would view it as a victory. But he would also understand the early leavers, and would not be offended. Irish people like to leave early.

Completion means nothing to us; we like to be ahead of the crowd. And the traffic getting out of here will be brutal.

Downstairs, three young men in suits are singing in harmony: 'Some day when the last line has been written . . .'

The girl in the camel wrap coat sings 'In the Loving Arms of God'. God would need long arms to get them around Big Tom.

I nearly break my neck coming out of the church, missing a step at the exit. The lesser priests are out in front of the coffin and the bouncer from the balcony is holding the container of holy water, with which the coffin will be sprinkled. There are six men under the coffin, all wearing Oram Sarsfields jackets. The two McBride daughters, Aisling and Siobhan, follow. Only the purring of the RTÉ TV van breaks the silence. The coffin, with a cross at each corner of the top tier, is carried down the path away from the church, and then up again to the steeply sloping graveyard.

People are walking on the borders of other graves in order to reach the spot where Big Tom will be buried, in the top right-hand corner of the graveyard. An empty wheelchair is handed up through the crowd. Once you are up on the hill, you can see that the crowd reaches right back, through the hollow, to the church. You can hear the sobs of the women at the graveside. And you can see the crowds on the hill on the other side of the path, where mourners stand against the yellow of the gorse bushes.

Phones are held up to take pictures of the burial.

A priest starts the Our Father. Then another priest starts a decade of the Rosary. He addresses Our Lady as 'you', not 'thou'. 'Blessed are you amongst women': it does not sound the same.

The graveside oration is given by Big Tom's neighbour, Jim O'Neill.

'The King is dead. Big Tom is dead. Dead before his time.' (Big Tom was eighty-one.)

'Thanks, Mighty Man, for the dances . . . Our local GAA club will be forever in your debt. You braved your infirmities and discharged your grand marshal duties at our St Patrick's Day parade.

'Bless you. Bless you, Big Man. Oram will always be Big Tom country. You put Oram on the map.'

Then he is finished. '*Ar dheis Dé go raibh a anam.*'

Someone starts to sing 'Gentle Mother'. Like most of the songs for which Big Tom is known, it is a weird swirl of the mundane and the picturesque. 'Some children take a liking to their parents . . . 'Neath yon willow lies my gentle mother's love.'

Now someone is singing 'The Land Where We Never Grow Old'.

We are clapping along with the music, which seems to exist in some other universe. It is clear that what we are witnessing is a graveside concert, delivered through a very good sound system. There are musicians everywhere, guitars in hand, working hard – 'Take it up a half, lads.' Now Ireland's biggest country star, Daniel O'Donnell, is singing Johnny Cash's 'Far Side Banks of Jordan'. Between the sharp blue suit, the haircut and the small glasses, Daniel looks like a banking executive.

And here is Susan McCann, and here is Philomena Begley.

Susan McCann sings the song that was her first hit, back in 1977: 'Big Tom is Still the King'. Tom McBride was barely forty years old at the time — not at all an advanced age in the world of Irish country music — but apparently there was a feeling that his status had to be defended. A second song about him, from 1983 — 'Big Tom Doesn't Play Here Anymore', by T. R. Dallas — was a lament for the demise of the dance halls: the big ones in London and elsewhere in England, but also the dance halls of Ireland, which turned into discos, then furniture shops or cinemas and finally, in many cases, rubble. One night at the Shamrock dance hall in Birmingham, Big Tom used to recall, 'the police came in and took five hundred out of the hall before the show could recommence'.

Philomena Begley sings 'The Way Old Friends Do'. Daniel O'Donnell sings 'Four Roads to Glenamaddy', another of Big Tom's hits. Everyone knows the words: '. . . four dusty byways to my heart'. One of the priests is clapping and stomping his feet.

Margo, Daniel O'Donnell's older sister and a great friend of Big Tom's, is singing 'A Love That's Lasted Through the Years', which she and Big Tom used to sing as a duet.

Down on the path, a couple are jiving, in a subdued way. The woman is wearing a turquoise top and the man's shirt is crisply ironed.

I'm losing track of the singers, because I can't see them. Someone sings Dolly Parton's 'Coat of Many Colors', which is all about being extremely poor, although the cars and the waistlines here suggest modern prosperity.

We are having a great time. The songs keep coming. This

graveside concert is beautifully organized, immaculately executed. There is no hesitation or doubt.

Daniel O'Donnell is saying: 'The family are here in front of Our Lady's grotto if you want to pay your condolences.'

I can't see everyone, but nobody in my vicinity moves at this invitation. Everyone is watching the concert.

Someone is singing 'I Saw the Light' – 'Jesus came like a stranger in the night.'

Someone else sings 'The Little Shirt My Mother Made for Me'. No Irishwoman has made a shirt for more than sixty years, and no woman here will ever sew one, but this music is about nothing if not nostalgia.

'Sandy will bring us home,' says Daniel O'Donnell, who seems to be in charge of everything. Sandy Kelly, once the great beauty of the showband scene, and still handsome, starts to sing 'Let the Circle Be Unbroken', and we're all joining in now, really belting it out. The woman beside me has a clear and lovely voice.

It's over. We walk up to the church gates and across the road to the community centre to queue for cocktail sausages and cake and tea. (Big Tom donated the land on which the community centre was built.) These are all served under a huge mural of Big Tom, which must be twelve feet high.

Tom McBride
1936–2018

3

The Body

An Embalming, Part I: the Artery and the Vein

On the table lies the corpse of a man. He is so neat that as I approached the mortuary room and saw first his feet and then his shins and then his hands and his bald head – the middle of him was covered – I thought he was a practice mannequin. The eyes and mouth are perfectly closed. They closed this way quite naturally, Patrick says, 'which is most unusual. Rigor mortis in this gentleman is very, very light. If you're a young person or if you're in an accident you can get very, very strong rigor mortis.'

Patrick – who asked that I use only his first name – starts to rub the body with moisturizing lotion. He massages the arms because, he says, even a little rigor mortis can cause the muscles to contract, which makes it harder to get at the blood vessels.

Yesterday this man was alive, and in hospital, and now he is a silent thing. Patrick speaks of him affectionately. He is 'the gentleman', or 'the boy'.

Patrick knows people who can embalm a body in forty-five minutes, but that wouldn't suit him. He likes to work more slowly, over about two hours. This body is what is called a 'trade case'. In other words, Patrick has been subcontracted by another undertaker, who will be burying the corpse.

I am quite nervous that I will faint, or vomit. I am imagining the room awash with bodily fluids. Patrick is wearing a black rubber gown, and at the back you can see that he is wearing nice jeans. On his hands are black gloves. The head of the dead man is on a headrest.

The embalming fluid – about six litres – goes in via the carotid artery. Meanwhile, the blood – about eight pints – is drained via the jugular vein. To access both the carotid artery and the jugular vein, you make an incision just above the collarbone. It takes Patrick a little while to access the jugular. 'I'm under a bit of pressure here maybe,' he says. He means because I am in the room with him. 'I'm normally here with Ryan Tubridy and myself,' he says. The radio is not on today.

The cover is now off the body and I can see a little hole on the right-hand side of the lower chest, with some tubes coming out of it: these were inserted at the hospital, to deliver medicine. Patrick removes them. This slim man looks like something from a science-fiction film, as if he might rise at any minute to find himself on a strange planet.

'I have to be extra careful in case I rupture it,' says Patrick, who is still looking for the vein. 'This doesn't happen a lot.'

We can hear the breath of the cars as they pass on the street outside. The frosted windows give a clear white light, and overhead are fluorescent bulbs. On the wall is a framed anatomical diagram of the human circulatory system. It came from a company in Wisconsin.

Having got access to the blood vessels, Patrick hands me a bottle labelled 'Dodge Chroma Pink 5'. It is full of an opaque pink liquid. Then he hands me a smaller bottle with a more translucent pink liquid, and this has a higher index: 36. 'They're all formaldehyde-based. But I'm not using a very high percentage of formaldehyde.'

Patrick is anxious. 'I wouldn't be the coolest person you've ever met.'

I wouldn't be the coolest you ever met either, I should have said.

Patrick has already mopped the incision once or twice. 'Oedema,' he says. 'There's going to be an awful lot of fluid on the loose in the body.'

He raises one of the dead man's arms and puts a black tube across his chest, with something attached to it that looks a bit like a dentist's drill. The silver Dodge embalming machine beside him had been humming but it now goes silent, emitting only rhythmic clicks.

Some people would wait until this process was over to resume work on the body, he says, 'But I prefer to be clicking away myself.'

He is cleaning the dead man's nails. He takes something away from the side of the man's mouth.

In the small town where Patrick was born, he tells me, there are still shopkeepers who close the door and put out the light when a funeral cortège passes. After a funeral, the first question asked is 'Who was under the coffin?' In other words, who carried the coffin?

Wake Amusements

As Patrick's question indicates, death is an intensely social phenomenon in Ireland. Until the pandemic changed everything, it was normal to go to the house of the deceased or to the funeral home, where the corpse lay in its coffin and where mourners would queue to shake hands with the bereaved family and drink endless cups of tea – or white wine for the ladies – and eat a limitless supply of sandwiches, or perhaps vol-au-vents, and chat with neighbours. And then, after the funeral party had accompanied the corpse to the graveyard – on foot if you were in the country, by sitting in heavy traffic if you were in the city – you would assemble in the local hotel or golf club for a lunch at a series of large tables, not unlike at a wedding, and frequently with a free bar.

There is no strict definition of the Irish wake – it can refer to almost any social interaction associated with a death. But the classic image – open coffin in the middle of the room, mourners mirthfully toasting the dead – has deep roots in Irish culture. The old Irish wakes were carnivals and satires, they were talent competitions, they were matchmaking festivals (to put it politely) and they were fights. Catholic Church authorities spent centuries trying to suppress them, threatening those who took part in them with the withholding of sacraments and even excommunication – to no discernible avail until around the middle of the nineteenth century, when the Church's ideas of respectability started to become culturally dominant. Still, as late as 1927, the Synod of Maynooth felt it necessary to outlaw immodest behaviour in the presence of a corpse.

No one knows quite where the wild Irish wake came from. Modern writers have connected it to the 'games of lamentation' (*na cluiche caointe*) that are thought to have taken place on the death of a significant person in pre-Christian and early Christian Ireland. A death caused the tribe to gather, and a funeral celebration, including a feast, is believed to have been common.

In 1614, the Synod of Armagh issued an edict against what it considered to be bad behaviour at wakes, saying that the people who attended them were imitating their betters 'in the manner of wearing black clothing to express their grief and in the provision of a feast to those attending the wake and the funeral'. This extravagance, the synod thought, carried with it the danger of impoverishing the grieving family.

The synod was also unhappy about 'obscene songs and suggestive games' at wakes, but their edict seems to have had little effect. There were card games at the smaller wakes; sometimes, even into the twentieth century, a hand was dealt for the corpse. Broadly, the Catholic Church's objections to the uninhibited wake came down to two things: money (much better given to the clergy or distributed as alms) and sex.

Immodest behaviours in the presence of a corpse were not a regrettable side effect of the Irish wake. They were exactly its point. It is a common impulse to laugh when you are frightened or upset, and in Ireland at least there is a strong instinct to party hard in the face of death.

The traditional wake games – often overseen by a sort of master of ceremonies, known as the 'borekeen' – were exercises in mockery and the breaking of taboos. The Church itself was one of the objects of mockery. Wakes included comic versions of the sacraments, principally marriage and confession. In 1852, the gloriously named John Prim mentions a game 'in which a person caricaturing a priest and wearing a rosary composed of small potatoes strung together enters into conflict with the "borekeen" and is put down and expelled from the room by direction of the latter'.

The customs of the wake differed, of course, across time and space, and from family to family. But it is possible to make a few generalizations, as Gearóid Ó Crualaoich does in his study of what he calls the 'merry wake'. The dead person's body was laid out in an open coffin, often in a barn, so that there would be enough space for the crowd of visitors. Snuff, pipe tobacco and tea were provided by the bereaved family. The tobacco might be carried in a bodhrán, a drum still used in Irish traditional music today. Wakes could go on for two or three days, depending on what time of day the person had died. (A morning death meant a three-day wake, whereas an evening death was followed by just two days of revelry – and it is said that young people implored old people to be sure to die in the morning.) The corpse was never left alone. The old people came during the day, and the young people kept the vigil going at night. 'A wake in Ireland is a midnight meeting,' wrote Maria Edgeworth, 'held professedly for the indulgence of holy sorrow, but usually it is converted into orgies of unholy joy.'

William Carleton, born into the Catholic peasantry in south Tyrone in 1794, knew the wake culture at first hand, and wrote that he, like the other young people of his district, 'would travel five miles' to attend a wake. 'That many runaway marriages resulted from them is a well-known fact . . . at that period of which I write more than one half of the marriages of the parish were runaway.' He lists the wake games of his youth: the Sitting Brogue; the Standing Brogue; Frimsey Framsey (a kissing game); Marrying; the White Cockade; Weds and Forfeits; the Priest of the Parish; Horns or the Painter; the Silly Oul Man.

Many of the games seem to have been little more than permission for what modern Irish people call messing. Croosting, for example, involved pelting people with small pieces of turf. There were games of forfeit, of riddles and tongue-twisters, and, for the young men, contests of endurance, strength and agility. There was storytelling from the old people, which was often about the history of the locality. Some of the games featured mock courts: Good Judge, Bad Judge, and the Police Game.

In 1794, an anonymous contributor to *Anthologica Hibernica* wrote that 'The vulgar Irish of the present day exhibit, in many parts of the Kingdom, several awkward attempts at comedy at their own weddings and wakes. These pieces are called: 1. Cottoning of the Frieze; 2. The Marriage Act; 3. The Servants Serving Their Lord at Table; 4. The Fulling or Thickening of the Cloth; 5. Sir Sop, or the Knight of Straw.'

The purpose of the Sir Sop game, apparently, was to 'hold up to ridicule the English character, and cannot therefore be a production of high antiquity'. Sir Sop was dressed in straw, with a cap also made of straw, while the Irish chieftain, 'who always takes his name from the Irish family of most consequence in the neighbourhood . . . is clad in the best clothes that the wardrobes of his rustic audience can afford. The dialogue is extremely humorous, and is interspersed with soliloquies, songs and dances.' Sir Sop was always vanquished in the end.

Of the sex games we know little, because those who wrote about them could not bring themselves to describe them, beyond referring to them as indecent. Selling the Old Cow, for example, is dismissed by the well-known chronicler of wake games, Seán Ó Súilleabháin, as 'a somewhat unpleasant game which often descended into coarseness'. John Prim mentioned Selling the Pig in his list of funeral games, without description of any kind.

Kissing games and matchmaking games were common. The most notorious of the funeral games was the Building of the Ship, mentioned by several of the Protestant intellectuals who wrote about funeral games in the nineteenth century. In 1887, Lady Wilde wrote: 'Details can very seldom be obtained, for the people are afraid of the priesthood, who have vehemently denounced them. Yet the peasants cling to them with mysterious reverence and do not see the immorality of many of the wake practices. They accept them as mysteries, ancient usages of their forefathers to be sacredly observed, or the vengeance of the dead would fall on them.'

According to William Gregory Wood-Martin, who lived in Sligo in the middle of the nineteenth century, 'The Building of the Ship was divided into scenes or acts.' He lists these as: the Laying of the Keel; Placing the Stem and Stern Post; Painting the Ship; Erecting the Mast; Launching; and Drawing the Ship Out of the Mud. During Wood-Martin's researches, 'When inquiries were instituted of one informant regarding the ceremony "Erecting the Mast" he looked surprised and said, "Lord, how do you know that? It is nearly sixty years since I saw it and sure the priests won't let it be acted now."'

Yet the Building of the Ship must have been hard to forget. John Prim was very upset by it. In his description of the stage of the game known as Drawing the Ship Out of the Mud, men 'actually presented themselves before the rest of the assembly, females as well as males, in a state of nudity'. When it came to Erecting the Mast, Prim primly explains that 'this is done by a female using a gesture and expression proving beyond doubt that it is a relic of pagan rites'. One would love to know what that gesture was. Another game, the Bull and the Cow, wrote Prim, 'is strongly indicative of pagan origin, from circumstances too indelicate to be particularised'.

And here we have a problem: the delicacy of the commentators moved to remark on wake games prevented them from describing them. The sweat and the screams and the

laughter and the adrenaline of the games is gone from us forever, hidden behind a discreet veil of respectability.

In 1938, Henry Morris wrote an article on Irish wake
games for the Folklore Society of Ireland (An Cumann le
Béaloideas Éireann), which he had helped found. Morris was
a scholar of the Irish language and a diligent worker for its
revival, and he remembered how, in about 1898, when he
was sitting in the Gaelic League office in Dublin, he had seen
a report from the Farney branch of the League, in County
Monaghan, proudly reporting on how Irish-language songs
were now sung at wakes there. 'But the Dubliners who had
charge of the press arrangements were shocked at this idea
of singing at wakes, and suppressed this part of the report.'

Seán Ó Súilleabháin, who published his book *Irish Wake
Games and Amusements* in Irish in the mid 1960s, was very circumspect about what he reported. But one subject both he
and Henry Morris are very good on is the cruelty of some of
the wake games: how a foolish boy would be mocked and
tricked, or how a poor fool would be wrapped in straw for a
game called Bees Gathering Honey, only to be drenched in
water by the bees played by his peers. Morris writes of a
game called All Around Your Daddy, in which the players
had to imitate what the leader did: 'If Daddy were a nasty
sort of fellow, as he often was, and gave out unbecoming
orders, the games were stopped by a relative of the corpse.'

Ó Súilleabháin maintained that the riotous wakes of tradition had never reached his part of the country, west
Kerry – which seems like wishful thinking. He does, though,
remember the bishop at his confirmation in the parish of

Tuosist in 1906 encouraging people to bring the bodies of their deceased to the church the night before their funerals. This he identifies as the death knell of the traditional Irish wake games and amusements, for without the body, the focal point of the merry wake was gone.

An Embalming, Part II: the Trocar

Patrick is gently massaging the neck of the dead man. He has put a mat of dampened cotton wool over each of the man's eyes.

'That's a little thing of my own,' he says. 'A lot of people don't agree with it.' The eyes dehydrate after you die, and this is one of the reasons the lids can pull back over the eyeballs.

'I think the colour is actually coming back into his hands,' Patrick says.

Embalming and other methods of corpse preservation have been practised for millennia. The Chinchorro people of the Atacama Desert in South America were mummifying dead bodies – including those of children, newborns and foetuses – some 7,000 years ago. The Egyptians were embalming bodies some 5,700 years ago. These cultures were aiming to preserve the bodies of the dead for the next phase of their existence in another world.

In contemporary Ireland, the cultural purpose of embalming is to make it possible for the body to be displayed in an open coffin without discernible signs of decay. It is widely practised here even though the period from death to burial is usually very brief. If you ask funeral directors about it, they routinely say that embalming is 'for the family'.

Now there's liquid coming out of the mouth of the dead man, and Patrick is mopping it, watching it come, mopping again: like a mother with a sick child. 'It's just there's so much liquid in him and we're adding more.'

He sets up a suction pump to collect the fluid. The head trembles: this is the only moment of the entire procedure that I find disturbing.

The worst funeral is that of a young mother, Patrick says. If you have kids there, saying goodbye to their mother, that would pull at you.

He checks the carotid vein. You can get clots sometimes, he says.

The small pump is now receiving liquid that is a lively red. Coming from the lung, Patrick says. You know by the colour. If it was from the gut, it would be quite a dark, chocolatey colour.

He's tying off the artery. It is 10.35, over an hour since we started. Patrick says he's going slow. The pooling blood is clearing. He makes a second incision on the other side of the dead man's neck, the left, where there is still discoloration.

Then he holds up an implement. 'Trocar,' he says. 'This is where it gets invasive.'

The trocar has a long awl at its tip, to puncture the skin, and a tube for collecting fluid. 'I'm going to have to aspirate all the hollow organs. There's no blood vessels in the hollow parts. I'm going to have to take out all the fluid. There's some liquid there already. Some of it I've put in. But I know there's a big build-up of liquid in this man's case.'

He punches an incision just below the man's diaphragm. The trocar goes in.

Patrick is opening the window. 'I do suspect we will have a very strong odour,' he says. The tube goes between the man's knees, snaking onto his stomach. Patrick is mopping a mustard-yellow liquid now. 'Bile,' he says.

He repeats the trocar procedure at multiple places on the man's torso, removing fluid from various organs. There is less of it than he anticipated.

When he is done with the trocar, he threads a curved needle. He is going to close the incisions he has made, below the diaphragm and on either side of the neck.

He pulls out a clamp. He's at the neck now. He's finding the hole he cut in the artery and then he will suture over it. 'That's a difficult job.'

It's time for a break. We go outside and have coffee. There are three types of biscuit: 'I am fussy,' says Patrick. I have two sticks of shortbread. Patrick has one. He is watching his weight.

The Website

Irish death ritual has a peculiar genius for absorbing new technologies in a seamless way, without anyone thinking – even for a moment – that it is departing from tradition. These changes have sometimes been incorporated despite the resistance of the churches and the funeral industry itself.

In 2005, Dympna Coleman, a native of Dundalk, was living abroad. On a trip home she met an old friend from school. 'I hadn't seen her for some time, and she said to me, "You probably heard that my father died." And I hadn't.'

'Later, my brother and I were chatting over the kitchen table with a glass of wine and I suggested the name RIP.ie, jokingly. We only adopted the name later; it's very short and easy to remember and it speaks to the subject matter. I looked it up to see if it was taken and I was very surprised that it was available.'

At the time of that conversation between Dympna Coleman and her brother Jay, two of the Coleman siblings were living away and three at home. They all understood that death and funerals unite a community. As well as their farm, the Coleman family owned a large pub on the Castleblayney Road. Their mother was a member of the Irish Countrywomen's Association, and an assiduous attender of funerals. So no one had to tell Dympna and Jay about either the traditions or the changes in Irish society.

'In Ireland we're quite preoccupied with deaths and funerals,' Dympna says. 'It's fiercely important for people to attend funerals – and then of course people are obliged to reciprocate, if someone has attended the funeral of one of your family.'

There are many jokes about the stereotypical Irish mammy scanning the death notices in the newspaper first thing in the morning and then ringing people up: 'You'll never guess who's dead.' Newspapers still publish death notices, and local radio stations read them out. But RIP.ie became a one-stop shop, offering services that newspapers and radio stations couldn't, covering the entire country and easily searchable. It is now so central to the business of Irish death that geographers trying to calculate how many excess deaths there had been in April 2020, at the beginning of the COVID pandemic, created their data set from notices on the site. In their study, published in September 2020, they explained that excess mortality figures are usually based on official mortality data. Those data, in turn, come from official death notifications, which appear on average 63 days after the death itself. The mean delay of notifications to RIP.ie, they found, is just one day. To get a quick snapshot of the net effect of the pandemic on mortality in Ireland, RIP.ie was the better source.

There are two types of visitors to the site: searchers who have a specific enquiry, and browsers who look every day, sometimes two or three times per day. 'Mondays are the busiest day,' Dympna says. 'Saturdays is the low traffic. Nine a.m. is peak time, when people get to work. We offer an alert service. For example, if you know a colleague's surname, or the town they're from, you can set an alert for when their relative dies.'

The website is a riot of buff and brown – tones that might put you in mind of the pale varnish of a coffin in pine or oak. Visually it is dull, dependable, reliable. Functionally, it offers services above and beyond what a newspaper or radio station can provide. You can send your message of condolence from New Zealand. You can look at a map showing exactly where the funeral will be held. You can order flowers, or a Mass card. You can find out about headstones. You can even get advice about making a will. The bereaved family can also post acknowledgements of people's messages and kindness, and notifications of the Month's Mind Mass and the anniversary of the death.

Occasionally – I would say very occasionally – the condolences section tells you something you didn't know. A friend of mine, looking at the page for a distant relative some days after attending her funeral, saw a message left by a distant cousin. It was signed by the cousin and his male partner. 'No big deal, but it was news to me.'

The website gets huge traffic, but it was not always so: RIP.ie was not an instant success. 'In the early days, it was horrific,' Dympna says.

The Colemans were, perhaps, a little bit ahead of the technological curve. 'Smartphones weren't that common then. Only three or four of the funeral directors had email, and only two or three had websites.' They visited funeral directors and encountered a fair amount of scepticism. 'Up to then they'd had a very clear way of communicating deaths – the newspaper, and rural radio stations were essential. People said, "There's no need for this." They had a formula that worked. It didn't make sense to them.'

The Colemans realized that they had to meet the funeral directors halfway. 'We knew by the expressions on their faces that they were afraid. So we arranged that they could fax us or they could phone us with the death announcement.

Those who were able to emailed us. There was a lot of hand-holding. We were very, very available.'

Dympna and Jay attended the Irish Federation of Funeral Directors' trade show, which is held every two years. 'That was very important because they just thought the internet was all pornography – and I don't blame them.'

A key attribute of RIP.ie was that the details of a death notice could be changed easily. In the confusion of grief, relatives can be left out of the original announcement. Mass times change. Sometimes a partner can even die in the days after the initial death. The funeral directors liked the ability to correct a death notice, but they were still in unfamiliar territory. 'At first people would type "HELLO? AM I THROUGH TO THE INTERNET?" We were so delighted that we'd type "YES" . . .'

An Embalming, Part III: Clothes and Sheets

When we return to the embalming room, the dead man is waiting patiently for us.

The embalming, as such, is more or less over. Patrick is suturing the incisions from the inside, below the surface of the skin. The thread glows white against the dull colours of the wounds. He puts a little stitch in the hole left by the medicine portal in the man's chest, then holds up a small bottle with a nozzle: superglue. He glues the skin over the incisions together, forming a smooth seam. The result really is magical: it is as if no one had ever cut into the body. He says superglue can cover a lot, 'Especially in ladies with low necklines.'

Next, using little blue spoons, he puts powder into the incisions to soak up any liquid. There were eight or ten stitches in each incision, he says.

He takes a length of cotton wool and uses a forceps to push it up one of the dead man's nostrils. A remarkable amount of cotton wool disappears – about a foot on each side. 'And you could put up a lot more.'

He has wetted the cotton wool with a chemical that repels flies. Some people don't agree with this step, he says, 'But it works for me.'

He takes a shower head on a flex from the sink and sluices down the table under the body. Then he washes the dead man's head. He lifts the man's chin. It falls away from his hand. This is an unsettling moment for me. For some reason I don't like seeing the head moved. Or how the body judders gently.

Patrick is inserting the eye caps: over the eyeball, under the eyelid, a bit like contact lenses except they cover more of the eye. After death, eyeballs shrink and lose their shape. The purpose of the eye caps is to maintain the shape of living eyes under the lids.

Now he is sewing the jaw. 'It's just one stitch. But it's one of the most important things.' His curved needle goes into the inside of the lower lip, which is very pale. Then it goes inside the upper lip. There is a brief glimpse of the teeth, which are strong and look healthy. No blood and no pain.

Keeping the mouth closed is an issue for embalmers and

funeral directors. 'Rigor mortis passes off the same way it comes on.' In other words, the muscles of the face and jaw could suddenly relax and the mouth could fall open. In hospitals they use a little frame to keep it closed, Patrick says, and he takes a beige frame from one of his cupboards. But he doesn't like the frames: 'They can leave marks if left on too long.' Some people wire the jaw shut, and Patrick has the equipment to do wiring, but he doesn't like that either.

Now he is opening the nappy that is on the dead man and is replacing it with a large pad of cotton wool. The dead man had a catheter; Patrick removed it when I was not looking.

Surely the catheter should have been removed from the body before it left the hospital?

'Oh, they do nothing,' he says in the tone of voice of a mother complaining about her children failing to help in the house. 'The bag usually comes with it.'

He is looking between the legs. There is dark brown shit up there.

Patrick starts to whistle. He gets a blue surgical sheet and lifts the dead man's legs to slip it under him. He is trying to pull the nappy out. It is the action of a million parents a million times a day. I say this to Patrick.

'A baby is relatively light,' he says.

He has a roll of lavatory paper now. He pulls the yellow bin closer to him.

This is the first time I've seen an adult like this. I'm trying to be a conscientious witness.

Wipe, wipe, wipe, goes Patrick.

'I feel very conscious. I feel I'm invading his privacy. Normally when I'm on my own . . .'

It's the vulnerability of the dead, I say.

'And they're trusted in our hands,' he says.

When the cleaning is finished, it is time for the modesty cloth. Patrick tapes a large pad of cotton wool, pristine, into place over the man's genitals.

Then he takes a blue scapular that has been resting on the table by the man's left foot. He raises the man's head to put it round his neck. 'Mary Immaculate,' says the scapular. 'At the hour of our death.'

He goes out of the room and comes back in with underpants and socks. He puts them on the corpse. Then the shirt: he inserts his own hand into a sleeve, and takes the dead man's hand and pulls it through. He fastens the buttons of the shirt with his black-gloved hands.

Then he is pulling a pair of jeans onto the corpse, which is somehow looking younger every minute. Too young to die.

Patrick struggles a bit closing the waist button of the jeans. Then he does up the fly.

The dead man's left hand is lying at his side on the table. His right hand and forearm are hanging casually over the side.

Patrick goes off to get the coffin and brings it back on a black trolley. He sprays the outside of it with furniture polish and wipes it. 'I don't know if he's finished it inside,' he says. Because this is not Patrick's funeral: another funeral director is in charge. Patrick likes to finish his own coffins himself — that is, to line them with what is called the side sheet, which is the white frilled fabric that tumbles over the coffin's sides. 'But that's me being odd.'

He now starts to operate the hoist, which has a ceiling-mounted track. He has slipped three black bands underneath the dead man: at the feet, at the waist and at the neck. He is adjusting the one at the waist. The motor starts to run, and the apparatus moves along the track. The dead man is lifted. The body gently enters the coffin. Patrick adjusts an arm, then pulls the corpse towards the foot of the coffin, moving the pillow so that the man is propped up slightly.

He is trying to cross the fingers over each other in a dignified fold of the hands. It's a struggle for a moment.

The dead man has no shoes. 'It's very, very seldom that we're given shoes.' The reason for this is that the convention in the Irish funeral industry is that the lower half of the body is concealed in the coffin. Patrick staples a sheet to the coffin at the waist level of the corpse.

I ask him if he covers the face. The rest of the body is clothed and tucked in; the face seems somehow exposed.

'I never cover the face before the final closing,' he says. 'It's bad enough having that thing going in on top of you.' He points to the lid of the coffin.

Patrick is not engraving the plate for the coffin. The funeral director in charge 'likes to do his own engraving'. He will engrave the plate at a little bench in this room.

So now, around one o'clock, it's over.

I don't have any nightmares that night. Perhaps because it was a job well done.

The Online Funeral

The pandemic, with its restrictions on funeral attendance, has seen the rise of the online funeral. You can log in at the allotted time – and sometimes there are repeat showings in the evening – to watch the funeral of a family member, friend, neighbour or complete stranger. There is generally a single static camera. All you can see is the backs of the mourners in the first couple of rows, and the altar.

You can sit and watch while having a coffee, or chewing gum. You can work on a Sudoku during the consecration. In other words, you are a voyeur. A witness but not a participant.

Most of the time it's a little bit boring, just like watching a funeral live. There are some novelties. If you start watching early, you might get to see the keyboard player and the singer chatting before the funeral mourners come into the church. You see brothers reaching out to each other on the front bench and kissing each other – something you might have missed if you'd been at the back of a crowded church. But you're still in your living room on your own.

Towards the end of one funeral I watched online – during the prayers of commendation, just as the men in the family were putting on their coats ready to carry the coffin out of the church – the cloud of incense that had enshrouded the coffin set off the fire alarm. The family had to carry their mother out of the church accompanied by its screeching, while the public address system played a 1950s number that had presumably been the dead woman's favourite song.

When the funeral is finished, the undertakers come in and take away the mementoes left at the altar. I saw one undertaker put a tiny statue of the Virgin Mary into his pocket for safe keeping.

A funeral in Clare, of a man I never knew, made me cry. The camera roamed fluidly around the church – even zooming in on the photograph of the deceased on his coffin. It's surprising what can move you. For me it was the son giving the eulogy, who halted after he said the simple words 'he would always wake up early'.

I was moved, too, by the priest, who said that friends and neighbours were waiting in the churchyard outside. And I was moved when, after the priest read Derek Mahon's poem 'Everything Is Going to Be All Right', the cries of seagulls filled the empty church. 'The seagulls are right on cue,' said the priest, who seemed so kind. He emphasized how the deceased, who'd died at home at the age of eighty-five, was just an ordinary man who'd led an ordinary life. 'Taking care of his family and taking care of the animals,' as his son put it. Playing a game of forty-fives on Friday nights.

As the coffin was wheeled out the door of the church, followed faithfully by the camera, I thought about his grandsons performing two songs for him today, and of how the applause of fewer than a dozen people can sound quite loud. And about how ordinary life can be beautiful.

The Washing and the Shrouding

Before the rise of the modern funeral industry in Ireland, it was the women who laid out the bodies of the dead, washing them and wrapping them. The prepared bodies were often laid out on tables – or, in south Ulster and south Mayo, on a makeshift shelf *under* the table – and placed facing east in the barn where the wake was to be held.

In Dublin today there are still women who lay out bodies, and the bodies still face east: at the mosque in Clonskeagh. The body washers are women in their thirties, all wives and mothers: 'Let the most trustworthy among you wash the bodies of the dead,' said the Prophet. The equipment is kept in a large lilac suitcase with wheels. Amilah, beautiful and efficient, is the leader. She did her first washing and shrouding of a corpse when she was fourteen years old. Today she is dressed in a beige hijab and a long gown with a small floral print. Her jeans poke out beneath its hem. The hijab and djellaba might get splashed, she says: 'You don't want to go home in them.' So the women remove them and work in jeans and T-shirts.

The washing of the dead, according to Sharia law, is similar to the washing done by the living to prepare themselves for prayer. It is traditional, but it is also modern. 'We use gloves, face masks, disposable white coats, plastic aprons and covers on our shoes,' Amilah says. 'We have towels and sheets to cover the body. A sliding sheet is used to move the body from one table to the other. We've recently invested in a hoist.'

Before the mosque had a morgue, the washing of bodies had to take place in hospitals and funeral homes. Once they washed the body of 'a beautiful seven-year-old girl' at the chapel of rest at Our Lady's Children's Hospital in Crumlin. 'That was a nice place to wash, so clean.'

It was her mother who taught Amilah how to prepare a body. The imam's wife had called Amilah's mother to come and help wash a stillborn baby, and she brought Amilah with her. 'I could have said no. The imam could have said no.'

Amilah and I have been here since eleven o'clock. The other ladies arrive twenty minutes later: Sabina, who is pushing her little boy in his buggy; Aisha, whose family lives in Saudi Arabia; and Chana, who comes from Agadir in Morocco.

We cannot go into the morgue at the mosque today because there are two male bodies in it. Men wash the male bodies and women wash the female bodies, with exceptions made only for the spouse of the deceased. More than that, women cannot even see a male body before it is prepared – or afterwards, for that matter. Members of the opposite sex can see a dead body only if they belong to the family of the deceased. This is why I have not been able to witness the laying-out of a body here in the mosque: all the deaths since I made my request have been of males.

So today the female team is kindly staging a demonstration for me. Chana is going to be the corpse. She takes off her hijab and her djellaba. Underneath she is wearing a T-shirt that says 'Kiss Me Goodnight'. In the meeting room she climbs up on the tables, which have been pushed together. Sabina and Aisha drape a pink bedspread over her.

Before the ceremonial washing starts, all make-up and nail varnish are removed from the corpse. Then the clothes are removed. Aisha mimes cutting, with scissors, along the side seam of Chana's sweatpants and the side seam of her T-shirt.

The body is pulled up to a sitting position. 'Then we press on their stomach,' says Amilah. 'This is the main waste. Then we wash that area, not looking.'

Down in the morgue there is a stainless-steel hose. The genital and anal area is washed either by the main washer or by a member of the family of the deceased.

'We take our time,' says Amilah. 'The men do it much quicker.'

The women make sure that the water is not cold. Before they start the ritual washing of the dead, they say 'Bismillah': in the name of God.

The first wash begins. The right hand is washed three times and the left hand is washed three times. The arm is washed up to the elbow three times. The hair is wiped three times. Then the right foot is washed three times and the left foot is washed three times.

The women wash the corpse's hair – they have shampoo and conditioner – and towel it dry. If it is long, it is styled into three plaits. Nigerian ladies often have hair extensions, says Amilah, and this poses a challenge. 'Unless there is a Nigerian lady helping us, we cut the extensions off. But we don't cut the hair or the nails and we don't shave the body.' The all-over washing of the body is with a substance called sidr, which comes from the leaves of the lotus tree. 'It looks and smells like henna,' says Amilah. The sidr is dissolved in water. If there is no sidr, they use a commercial body wash.

The right side of the corpse is washed first, then the left side the same way. Every wash starts at the top of the body.

Then, Amilah says, 'We roll them,' and she pushes Chana over onto her side, so that her back is towards Aisha and Sabina, who are standing at the far side of the table. Aisha mimes washing Chana's back and bottom. She holds a pink bedspread protectively over Chana as she does this, so that the body is not exposed to living eyes.

'We have loofahs and sponges,' says Amilah. 'It depends on the person. Sometimes their skin is very delicate, and we wrap cotton wool round our hands and wash with that, using water only.'

The second wash is done using water in which camphor has been soaked. Camphor, as well as smelling sweet, is a preservative. Then they towel the body dry.

Two of the women hold a big bath towel over the body and pull the now wet sheet from underneath. There is now a pink towel over the corpse instead of the pink bedspread.

To get a fresh towel under the corpse, they roll it longitudinally, place it beside the corpse as she lies on her side, in line with her spine, and then pull it out the other side.

Then the shrouding begins, in generous sheets of cotton. Five sheets for a woman, three for a man. (In Ireland, traditional waking sheets were also five in number, kept at one house in the community and never used for anything else.) One sheet is of a dazzling white cotton. One is cream-coloured, with a self stripe woven into it. This is Yemeni cotton, say the women. The Prophet himself was buried in Yemeni cotton.

After a female corpse has been laid on the outer sheet, a second sheet, the *sinaband*, is laid over her, stretching from her armpits to her thighs. The third layer is the *izaar*, which goes over the corpse's hips and round the hollow of her back, a bit like a cummerbund, to shield the private parts. Both male and female corpses wear the *izaar*.

The *khamis*, which is almost a garment, has a small cross-shaped hole cut in the top of it, so that it can be pulled over the dead person's head and then dragged down her body, front and back. (In Ireland there was exactly such a sheet – the *táiseadach*, or grave cloth – with a hole cut in the middle, to shroud corpses. The remnants of the *táiseadach* were used for cures for the living.)

Aisha's mother in Saudi Arabia – 'May Allah reward her' – has sent the pre-cut shrouding pieces that you can buy in the shops there.

They bring Chana's hands to her breast and fold them, the right hand over the left. They wrap the *izaar* from the left, and then the fabric from the right comes over. The *khamis* comes over her head and is tucked on the left side first, then the right. Sabina and Aisha bring Chana's head through the hole in the *khamis*, so that her lovely face is framed in white fabric.

There is an additional sheet for a dead woman – the *orhi* – which is tied round the head of the corpse and tucked under her chin, covering her hair, like the headscarves worn by the British queen.

There is a short pause now that the body is shrouded, with just her face exposed. Aisha says that at a previous demonstration, 'I wanted to be on the table' – being on the table is quite restful for a busy mother. Her friends took pictures of her as a corpse and shared them with some female friends, which led to quite a lot of phone calls from people wondering if she was okay.

It depends on the imam at each mosque, the women say, but the imam here does not like women to wash and prepare bodies when they have their periods. One of the women confesses to having broken this rule twice.

Now come the ties for the shroud. There can be five or seven ties, or three if the dead person is small. Today the body is tied at the ankles, at the knees, and just below the waist at the belly.

Once the family has seen the face of the dead person, the face will be shrouded under the final sheet. Then the whole shroud, which is known as the *kaffan*, is rubbed with scented oils.

Embalming is not widely performed on Muslim corpses, unless they are being repatriated for burial. 'It is such an invasive process,' says Amilah. 'The Prophet said that you should be buried where you die. Although some Bosnian ladies want to be repatriated.'

The women agree that the work of preparing a body is very satisfying. Sabina remembers preparing the body of a woman who had no family or friends to mourn her. 'We hugged her and kissed her. I was affected by that for a couple of days.'

The Keening

The Prophet's beautiful daughter Ruqayyah died when she was still in her twenties, having been married and divorced and suffered the death of her only child, a son, at the age of six. Muhammad returned to Medina and went with his family to grieve at Ruqayyah's grave. The mourning women cried out with a great deal of noise. The man who was with the Prophet hit them with his whip, but the Prophet said, 'Let them weep, Umar. But beware of the braying of Satan.'

For a long time in Ireland, professional mourning women were a vital part of the traditional peasant funeral. Sometimes they were paid with money, sometimes in alcohol. They praised the deceased in verse, extemporizing their songs: this was keening. They sometimes tried to outdo each other, abusing their rival keeners. They keened as the coffin was carried out of the house and placed on chairs. They would travel with it to the graveyard; if it was carried by a cart, one or two of them would sit on the coffin as it was transported. If the dead person had been young, the keeners would stay at the graveyard and keen over the grave.

The Catholic Church did not like this pagan abandon any more than it liked wake games. There were edicts against keening women in the synods of Tuam (1631); Armagh (1670); Meath (1686); Kildare and Leighlin (1748); and Cashel and Emly (1800). Still the women howled on. Seán Ó Súilleabháin, usually so circumspect, tells of how a priest took a whip to three keeners in Kilmacalogue in County

Kerry. The priest said, 'You would keen over a dog, you hag, if you found him dead.' To which one of the keeners replied, 'You make a good living out of it.'

The corpses of young married women – many of whom, one presumes, died in childbirth – were hotly disputed territory. These rows were remembered into modern times, as Gearóid Ó Crualaoich has demonstrated, by people who spoke to the Irish Folklore Commission in 1935. Where was a young married woman to be buried? With her husband's family? But surely the husband would marry again. A French traveller, the Chevalier de Latocnaye, was in Kerry in the 1790s. In the town of Killarney he witnessed the funeral of a young married woman, 'her coffin surrounded by a prodigious number of females who wept and chanted their "hu lu lu" in chorus, the men looking on rather indifferently. When the funeral arrived at the head of the "T", that is, at the end of the principal street of the town, a singular dispute occurred between the husband and the brother of the deceased.'

The husband wanted the funeral to turn for Muckross, where his family was traditionally buried. The brother wanted his sister brought to Aghadoe, where their family was traditionally buried. According to de Latocnaye, the coffin was put down on the ground while the mourners fought 'with blows of sticks'. Eventually Latocnaye's companion, Mr Herbert, an Anglican minister of the parish and also a justice of the peace, 'threw himself into the middle of the fight' and decided 'that the husband had the right to decide where his wife should be buried'. He restrained the wife's brother, and the funeral went on its way to Muckross. 'I remarked that neither fight nor controversy which followed arrested the cries of the wailing women, who continued to beat their breasts, tear their hair and cry "hu lu lu" as if neither fight nor controversy proceeded.'

The Anatomists and the Body Snatchers

Some people do not have funerals, because they have donated their bodies to science. After they die, their bodies will be embalmed and, in all likelihood, end up in the anatomy room of a medical school. After the mother of a friend of mine donated her body to science, one of the medical students recognized the dead woman by her unusual first name as they were being introduced to the cadavers in the anatomy room: she was her god-mother's mother. Ireland is a small country.

In the anatomy room at an Irish medical school I've agreed not to identify, two cadavers, one male and one female, lie side by side. The male cadaver is quite fat, his stomach arching upwards.

Tall girls summon the smaller girls – most of the small girls are wearing hijabs – to the front of the group so that they can get a better view. The cadavers quieten us all.

Today's lesson concerns the femoral triangle, a busy junction of blood vessels in the groin area. After much cutting, the upper leg is flayed and the muscles exposed.

Now we are in the subsartorial canal, or Hunter's canal: a

sort of tunnel in the middle of the thigh that houses the femoral artery and vein, and two nerves.

There is something sacred here. You can feel the gravity. The secrets of our architecture. The people here donated their bodies because they wanted to help, because they didn't like waste. Standing in this room, you think of dead bodies all over the world, and of past medical students who were known to use a section of dead person's intestine as a skipping rope. And you think of John Hunter, the great Scottish anatomist and surgeon, after whom Hunter's canal is named.

Hunter lived in eighteenth-century London. As well as keeping a menagerie at his house in Earls Court, he also had a huge collection of anatomical specimens, both animal and human. His patients included two prime ministers; he removed a growth from William Pitt's cheek in a six-minute operation that took place at Downing Street, and for which Pitt refused to be physically restrained as other patients were in those days before anaesthetics. Hunter trained many students who went on to teach anatomy and surgery in America, in Ireland and all over Britain. He is known as the father of surgery. One of the best sets of notes describing Hunter's idiosyncratic lectures was taken in shorthand by a young student called James Parkinson, who would later go on to identify what was then known as shaking palsy as the disease that would take his name.

All of this training relied on the availability of bodies to be dissected, and bodies were in short supply. For one thing, there was no reliable method to prevent corpses from decomposing, so the dissecting took place in winter and Hunter himself advised that anatomy rooms should always face north.

The new science of anatomy caused the creation of a new market in corpses. Burke and Hare, who murdered sixteen people in Edinburgh in 1828 to sell to the anatomists, charged £10 for a body in winter and £8 in summer, when there was less demand. As surgical science and training advanced, graves were routinely robbed in order to meet the demands of the anatomy schools. Everybody knew it. In her biography of John Hunter, Wendy Moore makes clear how implicated eighteenth-century medicine was in the body-snatching business. In 1793, late in Hunter's career, one of his last students, James Williams, wrote home asking for money to buy a corpse – the going rate was one guinea. There were riots at the gallows at Tyburn in London as the crowd tried to stop the anatomists or their agents from taking the bodies of people who had been hanged. Hunter himself knew that the touch of a dead man's hand was believed to cure tumours, and at Tyburn, mothers would brush the hands of the hanged person against their babies. (In Ireland, even the hands of corpses that had met a natural death had a healing power.) The anatomists were allowed the bodies of hanged criminals, but their problem was that there weren't enough people being hanged. Skilled grave robbers could harvest up to ten bodies a night.

The novelist Laurence Sterne, who died in 1768 at the age of fifty-four, was buried at St George's in Hanover Square, a prime hunting ground for grave robbers. Two days later, his body appeared on a dissecting table at Cambridge University, which Sterne had attended as a young man. Someone recognized him, but the dissection went ahead anyway.

Like many collectors, Hunter was obsessed. Carts trundled up to his London house at night, and the house itself was the model for the house of Robert Louis Stevenson's Dr Jekyll. Hunter was interested not only in corpses for dissection, but in unusual specimens. Charles Byrne, also known as 'the Irish Giant', knew this.

There were several Irish giants exhibited in England during the eighteenth century, but Byrne was the most famous. He was born in Littlebridge in County Derry, and his enormous height has been attributed by modern medics to a genetic disorder of the pituitary gland (though his neighbours said that it was due to the fact that he had been conceived on the top of a haystack). Charles Byrne was a nice man, who charmed everyone with his placid nature. He became a celebrity in London, where he met the King and starred in a pantomime at the Haymarket Theatre entitled *Harlequin Teague or the Giant's Causeway*. But by 1783, his show-business career had suffered deep decline and Byrne, aged just twenty-four, was dying. He had also taken to the drink, and had recently been robbed in a tavern of his life savings. He had asked his friends to swear that they would place his body in a lead coffin and that he be buried in it at sea, safe from the body snatchers.

Hunter sent his servant, John Howison, to stake out Byrne's modest lodgings at Charing Cross. After Byrne died, on 1 June 1783, the *Morning Herald* reported that surgeons 'surround his house, just as Greenland harpooners would an enormous whale'.

His instructions for his funeral were common knowledge, having been printed in the *Gentleman's Magazine*. His friends seem to have obeyed them, and their behaviour indicates that at least some of them may well have been Irish. They waked him for five days, charging all comers half a crown to view the huge coffin. Then the funeral party set off for Margate.

The journey from London involved several stops along the way. At one of these there was a barn. The undertaker – who had been bribed by Hunter – suggested that Byrne's coffin be placed in the barn while the funeral party drank in another building. Then, with some helpers, he unscrewed the lid, removed the huge body and filled the coffin with stones.

Byrne's body, hidden under straw, was driven to Hunter's town house and then transferred in a cart driven by John Hunter himself to his country house in Earls Court, where he had a laboratory as well as his menagerie. The coffin filled with stones was buried at sea.

When Joshua Reynolds, Hunter's neighbour in what is now Leicester Square, painted Hunter's portrait in 1786, three years after Byrne's death, the great surgeon was posed in front of a section of a cabinet that contained the extremely large feet of an otherwise invisible skeleton. And when Hunter opened his collection to the public in 1788, Byrne's skeleton was one of the prize exhibits. Today the Hunterian

Museum is housed at the Royal College of Surgeons in London. Charles Byrne's skeleton, standing in a glass case, is still there.

A second Irish giant of a slightly earlier period also fell prey to body snatchers, but this time in his native country. Cornelius McGrath was born in 1736 at Silvermines, County Tipperary. He was soon exhibiting himself across Europe — in Paris, Florence and Venice. Like Charles Byrne before him, he had poor health and was frequently tired. He died in May 1760, after falling on the stage of the Theatre Royal in Dublin. Medical students from Trinity attended the wake, fed his friends on whiskey laced with laudanum, and took McGrath's corpse to the university. The next day McGrath's friends arrived at Trinity's dissecting rooms, where the anatomy surgeon Robert Robinson told them that the body had already been dissected. The truth was that it was still intact, and to this day Cornelius McGrath's skeleton is preserved in Trinity's anatomy school.

Patrick Cotter, a third Irish giant, was born in Kinsale, County Cork, in the year of McGrath's death. He escaped the grave robbers and the anatomists by being buried in Bristol at six o'clock in the morning under twelve feet of rock. He died aged forty-six, and left his mother £2,000. His remains were left undisturbed until municipal workers in Bristol discovered them in the 1970s. It was therefore possible to verify his height for the first time. He really had been eight feet tall.

The giants were of especial interest to the body snatchers, but no corpse was completely safe. Much of what we know about the corpse trade in Dublin comes from the scholarship of John F. Fleetwood. He relied in part on the reminiscences of medical men, who recollected the wild days of their student youth, when they had been on grave-robbing expeditions themselves. One of these was Professor James McCartney of Trinity College, who in 1828 told a Parliamentary Committee that medical students used to dress in rags to join the funeral party, and frequently carried a coffin full of stones to the graveyard. They gave the mourners a bottle of whiskey fortified with opium and took the body with them on a cart, or carried it between them as though it were a living drunk person.

In 1732, the gravedigger at St Andrew's church in Suffolk Street was jailed for collaborating with grave robbers. (They were also known as 'resurrectionists' and 'sack 'em ups'.) In 1742, his successor in the job, Robert Fox, was charged with the same thing but escaped before he could be tried.

In his autobiography, *St Catherine's Bells*, published in two volumes in 1868 and 1870, W. T. Meyler described body-snatching raids at Kilbarrack, Artane, Coolock, Swords, Merrion, Irishtown, Richmond and Donnybrook. His own mother had a horror of her body being stolen, and after her death the family guarded her grave at St Mark's in Pearse Street.

In November 1825, Thomas Tuite, a known resurrectionist, was captured by a sentry at Bully's Acre with five bodies. In the same month, a sergeant of the 73rd Regiment came upon a party of men who left six bodies behind when they fled. Earlier the same year, a party had been surprised in similar circumstances and abandoned eight bodies, some of which were already in sacks. It was said that two letters found with those eight bodies were addressed 'to well-known gentlemen in Dublin'.

Teachers and students of anatomy were not the only beneficiaries of this trade. When Tuite was captured at Bully's Acre, it was reported that as well as the five bodies, his pockets were full of teeth – presumably to be repurposed as dentures. Daniel Corbett, who was from Cork, reminisced as follows in his presidential address to the founding session of the British Dental Association in 1888: 'I recollect what attention was paid to the gravedigger on his periodical visits to my father's residence with his gleanings from the coffins he chanced to expose in discharge of his avocation. His visits were generally at night and no hospitable duty in which my father might chance to be engaged was permitted to interfere with the reception of this ever welcome visitor into the sanctorum of the house.'

Hair was also taken from the dead, for wigs.

The Irish were all over the body-snatching business in Britain. Most notoriously, William Burke and William Hare were both Irish – Burke born in County Tyrone, Hare from either Derry or Armagh. They had started in body snatching but expanded into murder, killing three men, twelve women and one child in Edinburgh for the purpose of selling their corpses to a brilliant Edinburgh surgeon, Robert Knox. Their trial, in 1829, ruined Knox's career. It was said that 25,000 people attended Burke's hanging – Hare had saved his own skin by turning state's evidence. And it seems a public hanging wasn't spectacle enough, for it was followed by the public dissection of Burke's body. A star surgeon, Alexander Monro III, wrote two sentences in Burke's blood.

In Dublin, the body snatchers serviced the export market, shipping Irish corpses to medical schools in England and Scotland, where prices were higher. Although this international trade probably started in the late eighteenth century, it was the arrival of the steam packet boats between Ireland and Britain that really blew it wide open.

One of the traders exporting to Britain was William Rae, a half-pay army surgeon who lived in Irishtown, near the port of Dublin. Rae ran a big operation, buying from other resurrection men if he was short of bodies. He stashed the corpses at a number of locations until he had enough for a consignment on the Glasgow boats. He was shameless, transporting the bodies in daylight hours and leaving robbed graves open to the skies. When he was arrested in March 1829, he was charged not only with digging up bodies, but with having them in his possession for export.

An Irish doctor writing in the *Lancet* in 1829 under the name Erinensis (identified by Fleetwood as Dr Peter Hennis Green, a graduate of Trinity College) remembered the grave-robbing expeditions of his youth. In an article on 'The exportation of dead Bodies from Ireland to Scotland and England', he worried that this international trade threatened to starve the Dublin medical schools of bodies. He predicted that the trade would ruin the reputation of the medical profession, 'the receiver being proverbially as bad as the thief'.

A Churchyard in County Wexford

For the funeral of Mrs O'Connor, I have driven out from New Ross with the funeral director, Joanne Cooney, in her big black car carrying the coffin spray of purple and white flowers and a framed photo of Mrs O'Connor, while one of Joanne's employees, Sean, has come before us in the hearse carrying just the lid of the coffin. Young boys, hardly teenagers, wear white short-sleeved shirts and black trousers and black ties. There are so many of these grandchildren, all dressed like this: they look as if they are with the undertakers.

Joanne and I drive on to the church, which sits on a hill about five minutes away, and deliver the coffin spray and the photograph. Joanne's father was from this area, and is buried in the graveyard where Mrs O'Connor – not her real name – will shortly be interred. He gave Joanne her first driving lessons here: 'I nearly killed him at that junction.'

Joanne's father, Jim Cooney, died in a famous fishing tragedy, the sinking of the *Pisces* off the coast of Wexford in 2002. Joanne also lost her brother-in-law and her nephew in that disaster, and two other men died as well.

Today, Mrs O'Connor's bereaved family will walk to the church behind the hearse. This is a common practice in the area, Joanne says. 'My dad used to bring me out here in the hearse to practise for people walking behind it at the correct speed. You put down your window and listen to the people walking, and if they sound like they're running, you're going too fast.'

At the church, the priest – I'll call him Father Tony – is getting into his people carrier. Joanne reverses her own car, and Father Tony pulls out of its way; this happens a couple of times before he can drive off. 'The cars are too big,' he says as he pulls away.

In the church there are discreet wine-coloured 'Reserved' mats draped on many of the benches. 'I got Mam to come out last night,' Joanne says. She looks good in her black jacket and black boots with a white shirt. A narrow black scarf is wound round her neck, a bit like a cravat or a hunting stock.

When we get back to the house, Father Tony's car is parked up against the hearse, poking out of the driveway. We stand by the gate and watch the butterflies bouncing off a big bush of buddleia. A fine floribunda rose, the sort that is traditionally planted at the gates of Irish farms, is leaning against one of the pillars. Its flowers are all withered on the stem. Mrs O'Connor probably didn't have the energy for deadheading roses this summer. She had cancer.

At 1.30, Joanne and Sean carry the coffin lid into the house, and some of the family come out the front door. This moment, when the lid is put on the coffin, is a terrible one, Joanne says.

The departure of the coffin from the house used to be marked by the coffin being placed on two or four chairs outside, as the families and the keeners had one last leave-taking cry over it. When it was taken up by the attendant men – relatives and neighbours – to be carried away from the house, the chairs on which it had rested were knocked over, and were left knocked over until the funeral was finished.

After ten minutes, a group of middle-aged ladies come out of the house, two of them sheltering the flames on the candles they are holding. Mrs O'Connor's husband is helped into a car. The hearse moves off, followed by Mr O'Connor in the car, and a group of about thirty people starts to walk down the road, with Joanne striding out on foot ahead of the hearse.

A funeral crowd owns the road; no one can say it shouldn't be there. It used to be the tradition that the coffin would take the longest route to the churchyard. There were to be no shortcuts: '*An timpeall chun an teampaill.*' Today, a warm summer day, we seem to be going straight to the church. I'm at the back of the crowd, behind a woman with tattoos visible at the top of her spine, above her spaghetti-strap top. She is also wearing black tracksuit pants with a stripe down the side – it is a sports luxe look for a funeral. People are chatting pleasantly to each other as we walk between the summer hedgerows. There used to be particular rules for funeral processions, like the one that stipulated that a pregnant mare could not be used to draw the funeral cart. Or that anyone encountering a funeral party should walk three steps with it in the same direction. These were known as '*trí choiscéim na trócaire*': the three steps of mercy, mercy for the dead and for the bereaved. But today there are no passing pedestrians, and everyone here is part of the crowd.

We turn for the church. Joanne is at the top of the hill and the hearse is at the church gates as we pass St Brigid's Well, with its reed crosses left by the faithful. There are dozens of people waiting to greet the coffin. The men of the family carry it into the church. Inside, Joanne is organizing the seating, making sure the old people get a pew. ('I'll kill Father Tony,' she says afterwards. 'There's people meant to do it, but they didn't turn up.') The church is so crowded that people are going upstairs to sit on the balcony. There are four priests on the altar.

Joanne and I walk to the graveyard, which is surrounded on two sides by open fields. In the old days the grave was dug, or 'reddened', the day after the death. Old people from Cork and Galway who shared their memories with the Folklore Commission in the 1930s said that no grave was reddened on a Monday: that was for some reason considered bad luck.

Mrs O'Connor's grave is covered with the artificial grass that funeral workers call 'greens'.

'It's very deep,' says Joanne. 'Because the husband is going in after her.' On the other side of the grave lie the relatives who died before them.

Most of the plots here are beautifully kept – a neighbouring grave has no fewer than six pots of flowers on it. 'The pattern's next week,' says Joanne. This is the local celebration of the parish's patron saint, in this case St Brigid. There will be a cemetery Mass next Monday for all who are buried here, so everything in the graveyard has to be spick and span.

We bring the wreaths to the new grave – at least a dozen of them.

'There's the boss,' says Joanne, nodding towards a fine

pale gravestone with 'Cooney' written on it. Jim Cooney is buried with his sister, Johanna, after whom Joanne is named.

The Mass is now in full swing. Joanne sits it out in the vestry. We enter the church by a side door as someone is reminiscing to the congregation about how welcome Mrs O'Connor made everyone feel in her house.

The vestry turns out to be essentially a kitchen. Sean and Joanne sit at the table, and behind them stand three tall candelabra, one in wrought iron and the others brass, with a phoenix and a pelican embossed on them. On the table lies the thurible, the globe that will hold the incense, resting in two halves with its long chains spread around it. It looks like an injured octopus. Beside it are an electric lighter, a long white candle, a used candle taper and a pair of discoloured plain steel tongs. There is also a brass jar that looks a little like Aladdin's lamp – 'The boat I think is what they call it,' says Joanne; it contains little beads of crystallized incense. There are also two foil packets of charcoal. 'When the Our Father starts, we light that,' she says.

On the draining board by the sink are two blocks of floral foam, some pot plants – spider plants, and begonias doing well – and a big plastic bucket with a blue lid, labelled 'Holy Water'. On the lid is a measuring jug.

As the Our Father begins, Joanne brings out two discs of charcoal. She holds one with the tongs and places the lighted taper against it for what seems like a long time – longer than a minute. From the church we can hear one of the priests calling for the mourners to offer one another the sign of peace. Joanne turns the charcoal disc over and heats it for another minute on the other side. When this has been done, she puts it into the bottom half of the thurible with a slight clatter, and smoke rises from it. She turns to the second disc. In the church, someone is playing guitar and singing 'The Old Rugged Cross'.

Joanne is blowing on the charcoal. Then she takes two spoonfuls of crystallized incense and puts one on each of the burning discs. The thurible is closed, with smoke pouring out of the holes in its lid, and she holds the long chains up with one hand while turning off her mobile phone with the other.

'After the prayers of commendation, we'll be going out on the altar,' she says. (Normally the sacristan of the church would prepare the incense, but the sacristan of this church is an old lady, and Joanne has decided to take matters into her own hands.) As we move out of the vestry into the side passage, we pass a framed photograph of the previous pope, Benedict XVI, lying on a chest behind the door. Two ladies are waiting in the wings, in the passageway, just at the entrance to the altar, the older one sitting on a chair – maybe this is the sacristan.

Father Tony materializes. He takes a tall cross from behind the chair of the older woman and hands it to a beautiful red-headed young man in a white shirt and black tie, who is as tall as himself. This might be one of Mrs O'Connor's grandchildren. The two of them vanish back out onto the altar.

There is a large, more comfortable room off the passage. It has a full-length mirror, and a drawer has been left open, revealing a garment in a rich red fabric inside. The room is full of the erotic thrill of getting ready, of getting dressed up. Outside, an Ed Sheeran song is being played.

Joanne shoots back in from the altar with the thurible, now thundering out smoke. She puts it outside the side door as if it were a smoking pan.

When Ed Sheeran is finished, Joanne and Sean walk out onto the altar again, and I slip out the side door. An old man trots past, smiling. When I turn around, he is tolling the bell, which hangs in its own separate concrete tower.

Around the front of the church, Joanne and Sean are rolling the coffin out the main door on its wheeled trolley. The males of the O'Connor family have decided it is too heavy for them to carry down the slope to the gate of the graveyard. So now we are all walking down the road with the coffin on the trolley. Sean is at the back of the coffin, holding on firmly to its ornamental brass screws, and Joanne is at the front, keeping it steady. 'The father's not good on his legs,' she says.

When we get to the graveyard gate, the men gather to take the coffin onto their shoulders. There was a time when funeral parties only went round graveyards in a clockwise direction. 'All right, lads, straighten up here,' says Joanne as they take the full weight of it. She walks backwards in front of them, then says, 'Right, lads, I'm going to stop you there.'

Six white linen towels are slipped under the coffin, so that it can be lowered smoothly into the grave. Funeral directors in Dublin don't take this much care, asserts Mick, one of the gravediggers. 'There's no one walking backwards.'

The men stand on planks as they lower the coffin in. The planks are to reduce the pressure on the grave.

In the old days, Galway people told the Folklore Commission, there was a tradition that seven and a half years had to elapse before a used grave could be reopened. There was also a tradition that the latest coffin to go into the grave should go on the bottom. But that's not going to happen here.

The graveside has always been a brutal place, and there used to be moments to soften that pain. In County Clare and County Cork, people used to put a bog sod on top of the coffin to muffle the terrible sound of the clay that the mourners threw down upon it.

Today the women throw long-stemmed roses into the grave. There is loud weeping from one young girl, then from others. Mick picks up the white towels and throws them onto another grave, out of sight.

In the old days, before the earth was piled on the coffin, the screws were loosened or removed and placed in a cross shape on the lid. This was to allow *cead a gcos* – foot room, or liberty – for the dead person in the next world, or perhaps on the Day of Judgement.

Afterwards, Joanne picks up the folded trolley and drops it, with the towels, by the pillar of the gate. Then the trolley is moved to its cubbyhole under the floor of the empty hearse, which now carries only yellow chrysanthemum petals.

I'm sitting in the driving seat of the hearse, which is now parked beside the flatbed truck that will carry the mechanical digger away. Mick and his colleague Donal still have to fill in the grave. People stop to talk to them, and to Joanne, as they leave the graveyard. In the pocket of the driver's door are two bottles of holy water, two biros and a packet of something that could be peanuts or crisps. The sugar-free mints are on the other side, near the gearstick.

This is not the first time I've met Joanne. On a previous visit, she told me about an especially difficult part of her job: sometimes it falls to her to cut the rope when a person has died by hanging. She keeps a knife for this purpose in the private ambulance in which they attend sudden deaths.

'Some of the guards are very good,' she says as she sits by the open window on the passenger side. 'They have the deceased laid out when you arrive.' She attends those scenes with her own body bags and protective clothing and plastic gloves. 'And we bring extra webbing for the lifting. If the person was very heavy, some body bags won't hold them.'

We estimate that the funeral was attended by about three hundred people.

The gate of the graveyard has now been closed. Mr O'Connor is guided to the front seat of a car and driven away. Refreshments are being served in the community hall. The old man who rang the bell has also organized the parking in the field opposite the church. This is Paddy Morrissey, who was born in January 1931 and reared in his parents' pub. There is no pub functioning in this place now. He helps out at all the funerals, he tells me through the window of the hearse. 'You can't get a young lad to do it,' he says of the task of ringing the bell. 'You can't rely on them.'

He uses Aine Kent's field for parking, he says, but a field is no use for parking in the wet of wintertime. 'We were going to get a new car park,' he says. 'But in fifteen years you won't need it. It's gone that way now. There's just one Mass a week here, on Saturday night. I'm doing this thirty years. Sure I'm sick of it now.'

Joanne arrives back with the lectern and the speaker system in its neat black case. Donal and Mick are bringing out the greens, and also a plastic bag filled with straw. The straw is used if there is water in the grave.

The coffin is now covered by a black quilted mat with a gold-stitched cross on it. When I ask for the technical term for this item, Mick says, 'It's called a pad. It's dignity looking like, you know what I mean.'

Because Mrs O'Connor is being buried on one side of a double grave, Donal and Mick had to dig right up against the large stone commemorating the others buried there. This double grave lies tightly between two other graves.

'Most of them round here are dug by hand,' says Mick. 'You can't get the digger at it. The grave we dug here the last day was by hand. It took from nine o'clock in the morning till two o'clock.'

They had to break the concrete on this grave in order to start digging.

Donal is smoking as he operates the digger. Mick is clearing the bigger stones from the excavated earth that is going to fill the grave.

'There's nowhere to tip the clay,' says Donal from the seat of the digger. 'So this is going to look terrible – up to the sky. The family have to take care of it. All the clay has to go back on the grave. They said they'll come back. The pattern's next week and it'd be a disaster – you'd have a whole lot of pissed-off neighbours.'

Mick flattens out the mountain of earth on the new grave by hand, so that it looks a bit like Table Mountain. The excavated earth is hard to cope with.

'Put this down in the book, Ann Marie,' says Mick. 'There's one person who never gets thanks – the grave-digger. They thank everyone, the funeral directors, Joanne and Sean, but not us. We're the first to arrive and the last to leave.'

Donal looks at the result of his work with the digger. 'That looks brutal, doesn't it?' he says.

'Cat,' says Mick.

The other grave was easier to work, he says, because 'it was an old grave so the clay had already been taken away. This one is a new site.'

I wonder what they eat during the long day.

'We don't,' says Donal.

'We get in and get out,' says Mick.

'We eat a lot of mints, don't we?' says Donal, and Mick nods. 'Mints is our dinner. And fags.'

The excavated earth is full of stones. 'Yeah,' says Donal. 'This place is as hard as the hob of hell.'

He flattens the mound of earth with the digger.

'Well, Mick?' he says.

'That's all you can do, Donal. You can't do any more.'

So the grave is now a flat-topped mountain that cannot be disguised.

Donal and Mick say that they are not ones for going out at

night. 'We don't be out at all, do we, Mick?' They're on call twenty-four hours a day, seven days a week, because besides their grave-digging work, they retrieve bodies from the places in which their owners have died.

'They won't waste an ambulance on a dead body – it might be needed elsewhere,' Donal says.

'We put on the black suits,' says Mick. They always have their beepers with them. 'If you want to go out, you have to let the others know,' he adds.

Retrieving bodies takes up quite a lot of their working life.

Mick has been working in the funeral business ever since Joanne's father first asked him to dig a grave thirty-five years ago. He is from New Ross. So people know him. People remember him.

'How could you forget a face like that?' says Donal.

They lift one of the corrugated tin sheets that they propped up to protect the neighbouring grave, and carry it to the flatbed truck at the cemetery gates. The clay on the grave is about four feet high. They lift the second tin sheet onto the truck, then come back and survey the grave.

'How will we make it look nice now?' says Donal.

'You won't,' says Mick.

They lift off the third tin sheet, then they clear the heavy-gauge plastic sheeting from the grave. One of the polished marble headstones nearby is warm to the touch, from the sunshine.

Do they ever think about their own funerals, or how they would like to be buried?

'No.'

'No.'

They're going to leave that to their relatives. 'And the Man Above,' says Mick.

They are replacing the conifer plants on the double grave now, and the grave ornaments that were there for Mrs O'Connor's relatives. Mick is washing down the grave and the main pot-holder with a hand brush and water that has become warm from lying in a black bucket in the afternoon sun.

He pushes the temporary grave marker, a wooden cross, into the earth, then he and Donal place the wreaths and two potted red begonias on the grave. Mick, with the eye of an artist, positions the coffin spray vertically in the middle of the side of the grave nearest the gate. Its purple lianthus and tiny rockets of pink buddleia quiver as he walks. The wreath spelling out 'Nanny' is placed at the foot of the grave. We count the wreaths: I make it seventeen, but Mick says it is twenty. He pours water onto the coping stones of the neighbouring graves to clean them.

He carries the new-looking sweeping brush with its red bristles and one spade and the black bucket to the flatbed truck. Then the digger goes on. It is a Wacker Neuson ET20, says Donal. They have a smaller one as well, that 'could go in the door of a house'.

In the country in the old days, Mick says, there were no professional gravediggers: graves were dug by neighbours of the deceased. And in some very rural parishes, he says, that is still done.

The two men light up cigarettes. 'It's a good thing, the work, we can smoke anyhow,' says Donal.

'There's times now when we're in the graveyard at five o'clock in the morning digging a grave,' says Mick. 'Then we do another one at two. There could be two or three at a time – one funeral at eleven and one at two.'

It is ten past three when the truck leaves the graveyard. Mick closes the gates.

4

Lyra McKee

24 April 2019

'Do you know where St Anne's Cathedral is?' asks the small old lady as we wait at the pedestrian crossing at the bottom of Donegall Street in Belfast.

I say I will show her. She used to know this area quite well, Mary says, but she hasn't been around here in years. 'I've come the whole way in from Andersonstown,' she says. Andersonstown is a republican area in west Belfast, about four miles away. 'God forgive me, but I hate them ones that done it,' she says. She turns to stand in Writer's Square, opposite the cathedral, where the crowds will later form.

Lyra McKee was a writer who operated largely through the medium of journalism. A member of the generation she called the Ceasefire Babies, she died in that most traditional of Northern Ireland settings, at a republican riot on the eve of the Easter weekend, always a flashpoint because of its association with the Easter Rising in Dublin in 1916. Shortly before her death, she tweeted a picture of an armoured police vehicle making its way through the dark streets of Derry. 'Derry tonight,' she wrote. 'Absolute madness.'

Lyra was a Belfast girl. She had moved to Derry – or emigrated, as she put it herself – to live with her partner, Sara Canning, a phlebotomist at Altnagelvin hospital in the city.

The two of them – the young journalist and the young phlebotomist – were watching the riot standing near the police and police vehicles. We know that the person who fired the shot that struck Lyra in the head and killed her was a member of the dissident republican group that styles itself the New IRA: the group claimed responsibility. We don't know who this person was or what he was hoping to achieve in firing the shot. (The fifty-two-year-old man who would later be charged with Lyra's murder claims he was only picking up the bullet casings at the scene of the shooting.)

The police put Lyra into one of their Land Rovers and drove through a burning barricade to get her to Altnagelvin hospital – Sara's hospital – as quickly as they could. But she was dead. She was twenty-nine years old.

I walk up the steps to the cathedral. This is a Protestant cathedral, hosting the funeral of a Catholic.

Suddenly there is a wave of sound, like the crackle of rain, coming from outside. It is the sound of applause: the crowd outside is greeting the arrival of Lyra McKee's coffin. The coffin is carried through the front door.

Many of us feel that no matter who is shot, it is always the wrong person. But Lyra McKee was the wrong person to a spectacular degree. It takes her sister, Nichola, nineteen minutes to say what Lyra, the youngest in their family, meant to them. Lyra's friend Stephen Lusty reads out some of the texts he received from her. They ask for his advice on opening the broken lid of a cider can – 'Lusty, you're an engineer' – and on chatting up women. Nichola says that Lyra used to call her disabled mother, for whom she was a carer, at least fifty times a day: 'Sometimes she was only upstairs.'

These chirpy details seem strange remembered here, in the vaulting cathedral, with the prime ministers of Ireland and the United Kingdom sitting together in the front row and the leaders of Northern Ireland's main political parties side by side behind them. This has to be the closest that Arlene Foster and Michelle O'Neill have been to one another in a long while: the power-sharing government created by the Good Friday Agreement has been suspended for two years, and Northern Ireland has been run by civil servants during that time. Lyra McKee didn't have much time for the politics of Northern Ireland. 'I don't want a United Ireland or a stronger Union,' she wrote. 'I just want a better life.'

Her TEDx talk about growing up gay in Northern Ireland – 'I hated myself for much of my life because of what religion taught me about people like me' – ended with an impassioned reference to the 2016 massacre at a gay night-club in Orlando, Florida, in which forty-nine people were killed by a single gunman. She wrote and spoke also about the suicide rate of her generation in Northern Ireland, and about post-traumatic stress disorder amongst her peers, the generation that was supposed to have escaped all the bad things: 'As surely as people from the Welsh valleys knew coal miners or Scots knew the taste of haggis, Northern Irish youths knew someone who was murdered,' she wrote.

When another friend of Lyra's, the Catholic priest Father Martin Magill, asks why it took the death of a twenty-nine-year-old woman to bring the politicians together today, his remarks are interrupted by a standing ovation. It starts at the back and surges up the church until it reaches all the important people in the front.

Lyra McKee
1990–2019

5

Mothers and Babies

Jennifer and Jess

Jennifer O'Kelly is a calm person. When I go to her house in the foothills of the Dublin mountains, she is not there. She arrives a few minutes later in her car: she has had to go and get milk for our tea. She is not rushed. Her tiny son Eoghan is holding a two-litre tankard of milk that is almost as big as he is. The baby, Lauren, is silent. It's just that her two older girls, Ava and Hannah, both decided to have cereal for breakfast this morning, Jennifer says, and that never happens: that's why she ran out of milk.

Inside the bright modern house, I am anticipating a conversation that will be constantly interrupted by a screaming baby and a resentful toddler. But everything is unhurried and quiet. Jennifer has unblemished skin and her hair is smooth. It is strange to think of her enduring any sort of turmoil. Eoghan goes into the living room to watch TV, popping back in now and then for a rice cake.

It is February 2019 – which means that six years and four months have passed since October 2012, when Jennifer and her husband, David, had to go to England to end the life of their baby, Jessica Grace. At that time, termination for medical reasons was not permitted in Ireland. Jessica Grace had no kidneys. She also had a fatal form of spina bifida. She had no chance of survival outside the womb.

Jennifer and David had been told about their daughter's problems just a fortnight before. 'There was no name for all the things that were wrong with Jess,' Jennifer says. 'I wish there was a name. I'm saying, "she had this and she had that". It wasn't chromosomal, it was just one of those things.'

Jess was Jennifer's second child – she had her first daughter, Ava, from another relationship when she was twenty – and her husband's first. 'His family was over the moon. This was going to be the first grandchild with the O'Kelly name.'

When they went for a scan at twenty-two weeks, the midwife said, 'I have to get someone.' Jennifer told her husband that this meant trouble. 'He said, "Why would you say that?"'

The bad news was broken by a consultant obstetrician. There was no hope that the baby would survive. The consultant, Jennifer says, 'laid it out to us straight. They were very sympathetic, but their hands were tied. The consultant said, "We can continue and I'll scan you every week until the heart stops. You can continue until thirty-seven weeks and then we can induce you. Or you can travel."'

Like every pregnant Irish woman, Jennifer knew what the verb 'travel' meant.

The medical team in Dublin gave them the phone numbers of two hospitals in England, one in London and one in Liverpool. The phone number for Liverpool Women's Hospital was circled. The Dublin team said that that was the hospital they were more familiar with. It was also cheaper.

Jennifer rang Liverpool Women's Hospital. The midwife

asked her to read out the medical report on Jess. 'She just stopped me after the first line, after "renal agenesis".' There was no need for her to hear any more.

During that fortnight before she travelled to Liverpool, Jennifer spoke to Jess all the time. 'I said sorry a lot. I was always apologizing to her: "I'm sorry this is happening to you." I wondered if it was my fault, if I hadn't taken enough folic acid. I felt betrayed. I'd got through the magical twelve weeks. I was only twenty-six.'

She and David shared the planning of the trip, with Jennifer dealing with the hospital and David booking the ferry from Dublin to Holyhead. They had been advised to take the ferry, and to bring their car, because it was a more comfortable method of transport on the return journey for a woman who had just gone through labour. 'You can lie down on the back seat of the car.'

On the day they were leaving for Liverpool, David discovered that he'd actually booked ferry tickets for the previous day. 'That just broke him. I said, "It's just a ferry."' But David was terribly upset that Jennifer had had to do everything, and go through everything, and that he had made a mistake in the one thing he had to do.

They made another booking on the ferry. They left at 2.15 in the morning. They dozed in chairs on the boat as best they could. Then David drove from Holyhead to Liverpool while Jennifer slept.

When they got to the hospital, they were given a private waiting room and they slept there. 'Really for two weeks we'd had no sleep.'

Three midwives who were coming off duty came in to talk to them, just to keep them company. They were angry that Jennifer had had to leave her own country. 'They said: "We're so shocked that you have had to come here. We're always shocked. You haven't done anything wrong." And that was the first time that anyone had said that to us.' Jennifer was one of three Irish women who ended a pregnancy at Liverpool Women's Hospital that week.

The consultant in Liverpool told Jennifer and David that because Jess was unprotected by the normal amount of amniotic fluid in the womb, and because her skeleton was so compromised by spina bifida, the pressure from Jennifer's body could cause Jess pain, or even kill her, during a live delivery: 'You're making the right decision for your baby,' the consultant said. 'She's a very sick baby and you're saving her a lot of suffering.'

Jess's life was ended by the injection of a foeticide, and labour was induced. 'I'd sent the nurse out to get another sick bowl, because I was vomiting, and I stood up and she slid out and my husband caught her. The first hand to touch her was her father's, so that was good.'

After Jess was delivered, Jennifer 'had that new mother thing, which was so bizarre because she was dead'.

The staff at the hospital, she says, 'know how to do death. I was in a labour ward and afterwards we were in a cold room off it, with a cold cot for the baby. They did her hand-prints and her footprints.' David's family had sent over holy water to Liverpool with them, and David had baptized Jess as soon as she was born: 'That was very important to us.' The staff gave them a little baptismal certificate, and a birth certificate, 'to see her name written down'.

There had been kindnesses in Dublin as well. David's employers had been very understanding, giving him time off without deducting it from his allotted holiday period. But there had been stress, too. At one point before they travelled, the mother of a friend – 'an ex-friend' – had told them they could be arrested for bringing Jess's body back to Ireland in its small coffin. When they returned on the ferry to Dublin, they saw a number of police officers gathered at the port. 'It was just somewhere that the guards hang out, at a filling station,' Jennifer says, but still it gave them a fright.

Jennifer had rung the ferry company to tell them that they were bringing a dead baby on the boat, or, as she puts it, 'bringing Jess home'. The company told her that if she gave them the registration number of the car, it would be let off the ferry first.

'They're so used to seeing us. We heard of one young couple on the ferry who didn't drive. They were given a cabin, all free of charge.'

Even though she was sore and tired, Jennifer did not sleep on her way home. 'I was awake. From the excitement of meeting Jess.'

Jennifer and David had left Dublin on Monday at 2 a.m. Jess was delivered at 9 a.m. They came back on the ferry on Tuesday at 7 p.m. 'Door to door,' says Jennifer, 'it was forty-eight hours. The same midwife who delivered Jess walked us out of the hospital – she was still on the same shift. It's strange, now, looking back, it's like it happened to someone else.'

*

One month later, back home in Ireland, Jennifer attended her first meeting of the campaigning group Termination for Medical Reasons (TFMR). She had gone to other meetings of parents who had lost babies at birth but she had not been able to bring herself to tell them that she had chosen to end the life of her child. 'I felt they were going to judge me.'

The women and men who formed the TFMR campaign group had been forced by circumstance to end the lives of babies who were very much wanted. Furthermore, in their grief they had been compelled to travel to another country in order to do so. In the run-up to the 2018 referendum on lifting Ireland's constitutional ban on abortion, when the general public saw the TFMR people, and heard their stories, they saw and heard people who seemed like themselves, who had been terribly unlucky and who lived in a country that offered them no help. Now, in order to bring about necessary change, they were showing their wounds in public. Unusually for people appearing on any side of the abortion debate, they elicited universal sympathy.

Jess had made her mother a campaigner. Jennifer's own mother was afraid for her, but she was determined. Her first public appearance was as part of a TFMR delegation to the Dáil. 'We went to Leinster House, about ten of us. All our stories were written down. So that was the first thing, but it was behind closed doors.' Later she did a radio interview and was amazed how many of her friends heard it. 'They all texted me. My uncle texted my dad. My dad had told everyone. His whole family was very supportive.'

Jennifer did not get any negative feedback on her

campaign work. 'No one has ever said anything to my face,' she says. 'Online is another matter, but we don't look at that.'

I think: this is politics, lived politics, right here in this kitchen. You don't see it very often.

When the result of the referendum came through – 66.4 per cent voted in favour of lifting the constitutional ban on abortion – Jennifer couldn't quite believe it. 'I thought it would be about 51 per cent. My husband was watching the television and he shouted out to me, "Done, Jen, ye got it! Ye won!"'

The TFMR parents went to the RDS in Ballsbridge, where the Dublin votes were being counted. 'We all walked through the side door. Very unassuming. We were never in it for the glory. Because we know what it's like to do it. You don't want it for others. Those diagnoses are never going to change. But how we treat them can change.'

One desired change relates to the fact that we don't have a language for the ending of much-wanted pregnancies. 'It should be called compassionate induction,' Jennifer says.

Suck, suck, suck goes Lauren on Jennifer's breasts, sometimes on one side, sometimes on the other; and sometimes she just likes to hang out and cuddle. She is a very calm baby.

Jennifer feels that her experience with Jess has changed her 'in every way. It cut away all the bullshit from my life. I would still have very little tolerance for fake friends. I'm a lot more grateful for things. We're in another boom now and all my friends are buying cars and going on holidays and I don't bother. There's just our family and our home now.'

We are talking on 13 February. Jess's due date was

12 February 2013 – six years ago yesterday. 'I counted down the sixteen weeks from the time she had been born. The twelfth of February was the official end of it. I got my period that day. I actually got pregnant that month. Hannah was born one year and two weeks after Jess's birth.'

Jennifer was now moving from the death of Jess to the birth of Hannah, and working and looking after her oldest daughter: she was in the midst of daily life.

'Hannah was a very tough pregnancy. I had a path walked to the hospital. I was twenty-six weeks pregnant on Jess's first anniversary. My bosses were great – they really minded me.'

Her fourth and fifth pregnancies, with Eoghan and then with Lauren, were easier.

Her experience with Jess changed her relationship to death. 'My friend's father died when I was pregnant with Jess. That's a normal death. I didn't know what to say. But now if someone dies, I can hold a full conversation – and I get it. The only loss before Jess was my grandparents and of course we thought that they were older than trees. I get what people are going through now.

'When I'd had Jess, one mam at the school just came up to me and hugged me and said, "I'm really sorry." She had lost a baby. A lot of people, I found with Jess, they just ignored me. When a baby dies, there are no memories, the parents have the only memories. One woman came up to me and said, "Your baby died? Sure you can have another one . . ."'

Jennifer keeps a list of her children's social services numbers in her purse: 'You never know when you'll need a PPS number.' She added Jess's name to that list, even though Jess will never have a PPS number. 'I always say "I have four at home", not excluding her.'

Ken and Caoimhe

When Ken Walsh's baby daughter Caoimhe died, he was employed at a BMW dealership, and the car he drove was a BMW. 'An S20,' he says. 'It was my demo car at the time. I carried Caoimhe out of the church and put her in the back seat. About a year after she was born, I was walking through the workshop at work and I saw the same car: it was in for its yearly service. That hit me very hard.'

Caoimhe was diagnosed with Edwards' syndrome, a chromosomal disorder, after her twenty-week scan. The condition causes some 95 per cent of foetuses to die before birth, and those few that are born alive generally die shortly thereafter.

Ken and his wife Linda went home to tell their two older daughters the news. That day Ken also had a conversation with his best friend. 'He said: "You can't fix this. There's nothing you can do." And he knew what he was talking about, because his wife's mother was after passing away and he had felt absolutely helpless. It's only when you realize that you can't do anything that you can look at what you can actually do. Which is to sit down in the evening times and talk to Linda, talk to the kids. Not to hide from it – because the kids pick up on that.'

The experience of talking about Caoimhe's condition,

Ken says, made the whole family better at sitting down and talking about problems.

Caoimhe died while she was being born: her birth and her death were the same event.

'We had spoken about what we'd do when Caoimhe was born. We wanted to bring her home. The kids wanted to have a sleepover with her. It was their decision.

'Caoimhe was here for one night and two days. And it was the best couple of days.'

Today, Ken and Linda are the Dublin coordinators of Féileacáin, the infant death charity, which was founded by bereaved parents. When a baby dies, the charity delivers a chilled 'cuddle cot' to the family: this helps preserve the body of the dead baby, and gives the family a chance to spend time with it. After Caoimhe died, Ken and Linda did not have a cuddle cot. 'But we had our families,' Ken says, 'and quite a lot of them are nurses. They brought ice packs. Obviously the colour of the baby is changing. But we took photographs of her with all the family round. The girls still call it Caoimhe's party. At the start we weren't sure what were good ideas or what were wrong ones. But bringing Caoimhe home was a good idea. We had Caoimhe in our room, and the girls in our room with us. All together.'

Family members and friends came to visit. One visitor at that time, the mother of Ken's friend Damien, had lost a baby forty years before. 'They were in there with Caoimhe,' says Ken, nodding towards the living room, 'for over an hour. Caoimhe gave her permission to grieve.'

At Caoimhe's funeral, 'There was a lot of crying, a lot of

upset. I didn't cry once. Now I'm the type of person would cry when Ireland won the rugby match . . . My times for being upset were in the car, if they played some song. Isn't it strange? I was still keeping it in.'

After Caoimhe's death, Ken noticed that people asked him how Linda was doing, without enquiring as to how he himself was doing. 'I'm not precious about it, but I did notice it.' He also noticed a hesitation to speak Caoimhe's name. 'People would say, "I heard what happened." Why didn't they say, "I heard about Caoimhe and I'm sorry"?'

Eventually Ken found himself saying to Linda that he would give anything just to hear someone outside the family say Caoimhe's name. So he asked some fathers who were members of the Féileacáin support group if they would be interested in taking part in a small campaign called 'Say My Name'.

'And to a man they said "absolutely". We got T-shirts printed up with one letter of the slogan "Say My Name" on the front, and the name of their baby on the back.' The men posed for a photograph in Stephen's Green, with their row of chests spelling out 'Say My Name'. There was an article in the *Irish Times* about them, and Ken was interviewed on the newspaper's podcast. 'And more people said her name. Normally it's unspoken.'

As part of their work for Féileacáin, Ken and Linda deliver cuddle cots to the Dublin maternity hospitals when a baby dies; and they talk to the parents if that is something they want. The hospitals are glad to see them. 'Last week I was in Holles Street hospital and when I walked in the midwife said, "Here's the expert." The mother had loads of questions.

Brainse Fhionnglaise
Finglas Library
Tel: (01) 834 4906

And then, when you go back to collect the cuddle cot, you talk to them as well.'

Ken doesn't feel like an expert. 'I'm always nervous. But there's little things can help. For example, that time Linda texted: "Mammy's name is such and such. Baby's name is such and such." So I'm able to walk in and say, "Where's baby Macey?" And go to the cot and say, "Oh my God, that's a beautiful baby."'

Ken doesn't know exactly how many cuddle cots Féileacáin delivers each year. 'Too many,' he says. 'Linda has done four in a week. I think it averages about one a week.'

He doesn't always feel like going to a hospital and meeting grieving parents. 'The last Bank Holiday Monday it was absolutely hopping down with rain. I was watching the television in my pyjamas when the call came. But then I was so glad that I had gone.'

Ken now works for Nissan. 'One time I took a Nissan Qashqai home with me. One day I brought it into work, and when I came back an hour later the car was gone. It had been given out to a customer in Castleknock. I'm on my way to Castleknock when she rings the garage and says, "There's something in the car." There was a cuddle cot in the car, and there's a plaque on every cuddle cot with the name of the baby on it. The customer had an absolute meltdown. But she was fine eventually. She'd just been afraid there was a baby in the cuddle cot, but of course there wasn't.'

Féileacáin also provides each family with a memory box. Ken shows me one of the boxes. It contains a teddy for each sibling along with a beautiful white crocheted blanket, a candle and lip balm, which the siblings can put on the baby. This is a way for siblings to engage with the dead baby, even if they're afraid of touching it.

'I wouldn't change what we're doing with Féileacáin for the world,' he says. 'I think we'll be doing this for the rest of our lives, and happily doing it. When you go in with a cuddle cot, they have their own Caoimhe. I'm there because of Caoimhe. I'm there to tell them things: like, if you choose to be devastated, you miss two or three days.' By which he means you miss two or three days of memories of your baby.

Every July there is a memorial service at a church in Dublin city centre for parents who have lost babies. Any bereaved parent can attend the ceremony, no matter how long ago they lost their child. Damien's mother and father attended the service last summer. 'It was the first time Damien's daddy expressed his grief. After forty-four years.'

My own mother and father lost a child at birth, more than fifty years ago. When I was out at their house after meeting Ken, I mentioned the memorial service to them, and wondered if they'd like to go. My mother said she'd think about it.

'You're never past it,' she said.

Tuam and Beyond

When Delia Mulryan was dying, in the care or custody of the Sisters of Mercy who ran the Magdalene laundry in Galway city, none of the sisters thought to inform her loving son. Peter Mulryan learned of her final illness only when he learned of her death.

Of the various wrongs committed against Peter Mulryan and his mother, this was far from the worst.

Peter Mulryan is a small man who is not exactly normal – he seems kind of better than normal. Inspiring. Life-enhancing, even in a hotel in Ballinasloe, which is where I meet him and his daughter, Trina. Trina interjects occasionally, but Peter is a fluent talker. He is proud of his seven children, all of whom have good jobs, and his eleven grandchildren. Before his retirement he had a good job himself, 'considering my education'. He lives in a nice house on a road out of Ballinasloe, a house he built himself and has lived in for most of his long and happy marriage. He is, you sense, the sort of person who would fix things for you, although he says himself that he has had a tendency to take the desire to oblige people too far.

Peter's talk is vivid. 'When I arrived on this planet,' he says, 'it was 1944.' He was born on 29 June, St Peter and Paul's Day – 'I'm called after it' – at the Galway Regional Hospital.

He later found out that his mother, Delia, had been born in 1911, making her thirty-three or thirty-four at the time of his birth. He also learned that during her pregnancy, the parish priest told her father that his unmarried daughter was causing a scandal, and that he knew a good place she could go, because she could not stay in the parish. That place was the mother and baby home run by the Sisters of Bon Secours in Tuam.

Peter describes his mother as 'vulnerable, a frail person'. Her family were small farmers. One of his uncles laboured on other people's farms and sent money home; another uncle joined the army.

'They had no car,' Peter says. 'They were very, very poor. My grandfather and one of his daughters, in the dark of night, they got two big bikes and they brought her the twenty miles to Tuam. She was seven months pregnant.'

Peter followed his mother into the Tuam institution six days later. He lived there until he was four and a half. His earliest clear memory is of the day he was collected by an elderly woman and her middle-aged son, who brought him to their farm. He thus became one of Ireland's 'boarded-out' children, sent from institutions to live in foster homes. The state provided a stipend for their keep. This arrangement provided foster families with additional income, and also, as Peter puts it, 'cheap labour'.

He was brought to his new home on 23 February 1949. He left the institution without having been toilet-trained.

'They put me in a van. My first time in a vehicle. They put me in the back. There were no windows, but I didn't know any different.' When they got to the house, he was afraid of the trees that surrounded it; he had never seen trees before. Inside the house, 'the walls were dark green and running with condensation. I remember the dog under the table . . . I'd never seen a dog before. There was a big open fire, which I'd never seen before either. And the bedding was white – so white. In Tuam the blankets were grey, and a grey concrete floor . . .'

The middle-aged son of the house, for whom Peter was to work, was a sadist. Peter used to dread the summer, because the man would put nettles down his clothes. 'He was a brute. He was even cruel to animals. I could never copy that; I went the other way.'

When there was no work to be done on the farm, Peter went to school. He remembers playing with the lice in his hair. He remembers the farmer mocking him for trying to look up a word for his homework.

When Peter was nineteen, he started searching for his mother. He phoned Galway Regional Hospital, and was told they had no records.

Years later, in 1975, he needed his long-form birth certificate in order to get married. He and his fiancée, Kathleen, had better luck with Galway Regional Hospital this time: a chaplain found the records whose existence the hospital had previously denied. The name of a village – Addergoole, a short distance north of Galway city – was recorded in the hospital's ledger of births. The priest advised Peter to go there.

Ireland's culture of shame around the children born to unmarried women was pervasive, but not everyone bowed before it. It was possible to behave humanely, and some people did. When Peter went to the village where his mother had lived before being institutionalized, her family were struck by his resemblance to them, and were welcoming. (Kathleen, who was with him that day, says they were also frightened.) They said they had even looked for him. 'I remembered when I was seventeen or eighteen I saw a man going down the road on a bicycle real slow, Peter says. Later I found out it had been my uncle. He said that he'd seen "a fine house and good land around it. I thought you were happy there."'

His uncle gave him an address for his mother in Galway city. This turned out to be the address of the Magdalene laundry.

When Peter presented himself there, he says, 'A big lump of a nun came out to me. They said not to say you were looking for your mother, to say you were looking for your aunt.'

On entering the laundries, the women, most of whom had had children out of wedlock, were treated as the most abject penitents. They had their hair hacked and their names changed, and they worked in the nuns' laundry businesses for no pay at all.

Peter had a fifteen-minute meeting with his mother, 'with the door left open so they could listen to what we were saying'.

After that, he went to see his mother about every three or four weeks. His mother, with her legs all blue from the detergent used in the laundry. His mother, who hardly spoke – the women in the laundry were forbidden from speaking to each other while they worked. Sometimes he took her to the beach, which she liked.

Then the nuns who ran the laundry told him that he was visiting her too often, that it was unsettling her and that they were afraid 'that she'd break out and come to Ballinasloe', where Peter was living.

He visited her after his first child was born. 'We left the baby on her knee. She smiled.'

His mother – traumatized, institutionalized and barely able to speak – didn't tell Peter the full history of her experiences in carceral institutions. It was only after her death that he discovered she had been sent to the county home in Loughrea after leaving the Tuam institution, and was confined there for ten years; and that his father had been in Loughrea at the same time. Like his mother, his father had been a member of a poor farming family. He was unmarried and presumably had been living in the family home when, at the age of fifty-five, he was institutionalized. He was fourteen years older than Peter's mother, so at the time of Peter's birth he would have been in his late forties. Theirs had been a relationship between adults – adults who were treated like children.

The single adult members of farming families, as Peter's parents both were, with no work or income of their own, often ended up living and dying in the county homes – as the independent Irish state renamed the workhouses that had been established under the Poor Laws. According to Eoin O'Sullivan, Professor of Social Policy at Trinity College Dublin, between the county homes, mental hospitals, industrial schools, orphanages, mother and baby homes and Magdalene laundries, 1 per cent of the Irish population was institutionalized in the early 1950s. It was not unusual for people to move between different types of institution, as Peter's mother had. O'Sullivan has calculated that one quarter of the women incarcerated in Magdalene laundries had come from other institutions.

Peter and his family later discovered that while his mother

had been living at the county home in Loughrea, she had become pregnant for a second time. Whether the father of this child was Peter's father, or somebody else at the institution, they do not know. For his mother, it was back to the mother and baby home in Tuam.

This time Delia gave birth to a daughter, Peter's sister. Marian Brigid Mulryan died in the Tuam home at the age of ten months, in 1955.

One day in June 2019, I drove with Peter from his home in Ballinasloe to Tuam, and he showed me around the dismal site where the mother and baby home once stood. The building itself is gone, apart from a boundary wall. The site of the institution's notorious burial ground, eerily, is beside a children's playground. At the end of the playground stands a high concrete plinth. This is a memorial to six Anti-Treaty fighters who were executed in Tuam by the Free State in April 1923. The site is ringed by the backs of semi-detached houses built in the 1970s, after the institution closed.

In the 1970s, children discovered bones on the site, but the implications of this were not pursued. Archival research in the 2010s by a local historian, Catherine Corless, revealed that there were nearly 800 children – including Peter's sister Marian – who had died in the Tuam institution but for whom there was no burial record, and subsequent archaeological investigations confirmed that the unmarked burial ground is a mass infant grave.

As a country, we were shocked by the way the Bon Secours sisters treated the remains of children who died in the Tuam institution, in part because it was such a gross deviation from

Catholic Ireland's reverence for the dead. There was not even a theological basis for this contemptuous practice, as there was for the barring of unbaptized infants from consecrated graveyards: most of the Tuam children would have been baptized before they died. Like many other relatives of the Tuam dead, Peter has been campaigning for the full excavation of the remains in the mass grave, and, as far as may be possible, the establishment of their identities and the causes of death.

In the intense focus on the dead children of Tuam, Irish society has paid too little attention to the survivors – like Peter – and to the damage done to them. Even the vast report of the commission of inquiry into the mother and baby homes, published in early 2021, seemed to hold the evidence of survivors at arm's length. Dead babies are much easier to deal with than live pensioners – and yet there is still no official memorial to the children. The unofficial memorial, at the time of our visit, consisted of a list of their names in a wooden frame leaning against the wall, condensation building behind the glass. The first names on the list, from 1925, the year the home opened, are difficult to read.

Peter's father died at the county home in the early 1970s. Peter and his daughter are sure that his mother's sister, working as she did in the city of Galway and seeing his mother perhaps regularly, perhaps from time to time, would have brought her the news of the death of her former lover.

Not being told of his mother's final illness was a fresh insult and a wound for Peter. He had reduced his visits because the nuns told him that they had been harmful to her. He bitterly regrets his obedience, and is furious about the nuns' failure to contact him when his mother was in her final illness. 'She'd been in the Galway Regional for weeks and the nuns never told me until she was dead.'

Peter and Kathleen attended Delia's very small funeral in St Patrick's church in Forster Street, next door to the Magdalene home. Delia was buried in a communal plot with a number of other inmates.

At the time his mother died, Peter's own life was really only just beginning. He was newly married, had just become a father and had a positive relationship with his mother's family. He was a good dancer: 'I never had to wait during a ladies' excuse me. Even though I was so badly dressed. I used to pick up the clothes that the Travellers had left in the road.' But it was years before he overcame his sense of shame about his origins and told his children that he had spent his earliest years in the Tuam home. 'When his shame lifted, our shame lifted,' Trina told me.

Driving Peter back to Ballinasloe, I ask him how, after what he'd gone through, he managed to be a husband and father. 'I was cold till I was married. Like that.' He points to my water bottle, jammed near the gearstick. 'Afraid. I don't think I ever smiled.'

Was it sometimes difficult to observe the contrast between his own childhood and that of his children?

'It's more with the grandchildren. When I see how they are treated, I'm overwhelmed.'

After dropping Peter back to his house, I drive round

Ballinasloe like a drunk. I end up in Roscommon. It takes me a long time to get home.

Unconsecrated Ground

If you want to find a cillín, you have to know what you are looking for. There will, in all likelihood, be no signpost or gate. It's best to go in the dead of winter, when the stones are less likely to be completely obscured by tall grass and wild flowers and brambles.

To reach the first cillín, we have to ford a stream that is flowing full after a night of snow. My very short wellingtons just about manage it. My guide is a local man, William. We are in West Cork.

We walk up a slight incline in a muddy field – all fields are muddy today. And here it is: two humble stones set together in the grass, with some unseasonal daisies quivering in the breeze around them.

William knows this is a cillín because the family on whose farm it stands told him so; we can see their substantial farmhouse from here, at the other side of the stream on another raised piece of land. William's brother was once in this field doing some work with a digger, and he asked the farmer if he'd like him to flatten out this mound. No, no, said the farmer, that's a cillín.

The plot is very small – about three metres by one metre – and William reckons it was 'probably just used by a couple of local families'. The flat stones are uninscribed. They mark the brief lives of unbaptized babies.

A cillín was where people buried bodies that, for whatever reason, were not allowed in consecrated graveyards: unbaptized babies; babies born out of wedlock; suicides; strangers; women who had not been churched after childbirth. It is the association with unbaptized babies, and thus with Ireland's denial of sex, that echoes the loudest today. There is an old and savage saying: '*Triúr nac bhfeiceann solas na bhFlaitheas ariamh: Aingeal an uabhair, leanbh gan baisteadh, agus céile shagairt.*' This translates roughly as 'Three who never see the light of Heaven: the Angel of Pride [i.e. Satan], an unbaptized child and a priest's concubine.' We are a lovely country. Scholars are aware of 1,400 cillíní on the island.

The Christian practice of infant baptism has historically been linked to a set of beliefs about original sin. For a long time, unbaptized infants – still marked by original sin – were deemed to go to *limbus infantum* after they died. The existence of *limbus infantum* was never an official doctrine of the Catholic Church, but it was widely believed. There was no getting unbaptized babies out of their limbo, no matter how hard you prayed. They would never see the face of God. Nor could they be buried in consecrated ground.

Under this belief system, frantic parents or family members often performed lay baptisms on dead or dying babies. In Irish, these baptisms were known as *baisteadh urláir*: baptisms of the floor, or of the ground. It was said that even mothers who had decided to kill their babies baptized them first, for fear the spirit of the child would return seeking revenge. A man in County Mayo told me that the men bringing dead babies to a cillín for burial – it was traditional that a baby would be buried by its father – would scoop water from the stream they crossed on their way and perform a lay baptism on the corpse of the child as they went.

It was believed, too, that if you stepped on or crossed the grave of an unbaptized child you could become a victim of *an féar gortach*, or the hungry grass, which left you with an insatiable hunger. There was also the curse of *an fóidín mearúil*, the stray sod or the sod of bewilderment – often, though not always, connected with the burial places of the unbaptized. The belief was that, because the unbaptized child was in permanent darkness, contact with its grave brought a contamination of the living, leaving the victim plunged in darkness in which he could be lost himself. In Donegal a skin rash was believed to develop on the person who had walked on the grave of an unbaptized child, even by accident.

Scholars have offered a range of interpretations of the cultural meaning of the cillín. But what seems clear is that, as the most formal method of burial available to the families of people who could not be buried in consecrated ground, the cillín was the site of a vast range of emotions and beliefs. For some, it was an out-of-the-way place to bury the unwanted or shaming baby. For others, though, there was no shame or secrecy, only love and grief. As any parent of a stillborn baby will tell you, we have not perfected a method of honouring their brief lives or dealing with our sense of them having died at the threshold between two worlds.

While on the Great Blasket Island in the early years of the twentieth century, the folklorist Robin Flower was approached by the father of a newborn baby who had died: the man was looking for wood to make a coffin. The whole village walked through the rain, 'all in a speechless trance of sorrow and respect', to the cillín, an 'unkempt space of dank, clinging grass, with stones scattered over it here and there'. This Blasket cillín also contained the bodies of suicides, and so formed, as Flower put it, 'a sad association . . . of those who had known nothing, and those who had known too much of life'.

Seán Ó Súilleabháin, in a paper titled 'Adhlacadh Leanbhaí' ('The Burial of Children'), talks about the practice of burying illegitimate babies face down if the mother was in danger of dying, or if the father denied paternity. The prone burial was believed to prevent the couple from having more children.

The writer John MacKenna has described how, in the 1940s and 1950s, his parents buried three stillborn and very much wanted babies. The burials took place in the back garden of a county council cottage in a village in County Kildare. The family left that cottage for a better one some years later. It was only in 1977, when his mother was dying and spoke of 'the other children', that John's father explained about the buried babies. He said that he never wanted to talk about it again. Later John told the new owners of the cottage that he had siblings buried there: 'They were very nice about it.'

While researching his map of Connemara in the 1980s, Tim Robinson was shown 'about forty children's burial grounds, only a very small number of them marked on official maps or recorded in any way other than folk memory'. A cillín might be located 'in some ancient earthwork whose origins as a stockyard around a dwelling had been forgotten for centuries and which bore an anomalous otherworldly repute as a fairy fort, or under a fence between two properties, as if neither side would accept responsibility for it, or on the no man's land of the seashore'. Robinson saw an analogy between these locations and the doctrine of limbo. Similarly, the archaeologist Emer Dennehy found that almost all cillíní in Kerry were situated near boundaries of some kind, and that more than half of Galway cillíní were situated near a boundary between townlands.

There is no evidence that the cillín is an ancient phenomenon. Like other Irish death practices, it may have been forced into existence by the collision between pre-Christian beliefs and the strictures of the increasingly controlling Catholic Church. The earliest mention of an existing cillín is in a letter from 1619 describing how an old graveyard outside Muff, County Donegal, was being used 'as a burial place for unbaptized children and suicides'. The scholars Colm Donnelly and Eileen Murphy hypothesize that Augustine's theory of original sin was revived at the Franciscan College of St Anthony at Louvain early in the seventeenth century. The Irish clerical students at Louvain, they say, 'would be the same young men who would subsequently return to Ireland to be at the heart of the Franciscan Counter-Reformation there'. According to this theory, 'the Franciscans, who were long established in Gaelic society, may have forced the creation of separate burial places in those regions where they were in a position of power'.

Cillíní are frequently located on top of older structures: what archaeologists call 'host sites'. Disused graveyards and old churches, for example – places that were already considered sacred, even if no longer formally consecrated. There was a practice called 'eaves-drip burial', whereby children were secretly buried by the walls of a church so that water dripping off the eaves, which was seen as holy, could baptize them.

In the late nineteenth and early twentieth centuries, churches started to set aside unconsecrated land, usually on the north side of their graveyards, for the burial of unbaptized babies. These areas were called *teampaillíní*, or little churches. It was within a *teampaillín* at Rath, County Kerry, that Emer Dennehy's cousin Joan Foley, who had died at six weeks, was buried on the night she died, by her father and her uncle. Joan's uncle was Emer Dennehy's grandfather. Joan had been baptized, and the family believe she was buried in this way because there was not enough money for a funeral.

John MacKenna has a more recent memory. When he was a teenager in the 1970s, he walked a girl home after a dance. Then he had to walk the eight or nine miles back to Castledermot. It was a summer's night, and at 'about four or five in the morning' he saw a man cycling towards him carrying a small box and a spade. MacKenna, raised by a mother who was from the west of Ireland, automatically took the three steps of mercy in the direction the corpse was travelling. The man on the bicycle seemed 'embarrassed, stunned' to see him. There was no doubt about what he was doing. However, he was not going to the site of the old ruined church, where John knew that the dead babies of his friends' families were buried. By this time, the local practice was that babies would be buried on the shores of the River Lerr. And so John continued on his way home as the man cycled towards the river.

The Abattoir

The two cows stand silent between the rails, one behind the other. The one in front is a black Hereford cross; the other, a smaller animal, is a pretty Charolais heifer. They are wide-eyed, the whites of their eyes visible. The abattoir is remarkably silent, perhaps because all the other cows, eight of them, are dead.

Their huge corpses hang from hooks inside. Steam rises from them, and the heat warms the room. Twenty more cows will be brought here today to be killed. We walk between the carcasses, and Stephen pushes them aside to let me through.

This is a small family abattoir, which supplies butcher's shops. Stephen is an open-faced, honest man who is trying to treat me gently. (Stephen is not his real name, and I've changed the names of the other workers: a condition of access to a world the meat-processing industry generally prefers to keep hidden.) I am trying to treat myself gently. We are both afraid that I might faint, and a friend advised me to bring a plastic bag in my pocket in case I vomit.

Stephen just told me to bring wellingtons. He gives me a white coat and a hairnet, to match the uniform he is wearing. There are a few pale bloodstains on the floor of the changing room. He leads me past neat forests of carcasses to the room where the men are working, skinning the dead cows and dismembering them.

On what looks like a clothes rack hangs the offal. Eight tongues on the top line, then hearts underneath, and at the bottom, enormous livers. 'They have to be inspected by the vet,' says Stephen. 'He's been here already and he'll be back before dinner.' The livers are eighteen inches or maybe two feet long. I remember my grandmother pressing cow's tongue with a weight placed on top of a plate. But these tongues will be pickled.

We step around the black and white head of a cow that is lying on the floor.

There is a man on top of a sort of scaffold working on a dead cow that is suspended from the ceiling. He's taking off the black and white hide. 'David's just legging it now,' says Stephen. 'That's removing the hind legs.' Which I don't want to see.

Yesterday they were killing cattle and sheep; today it is cattle, and tomorrow it is pigs and sheep.

There is another three-level rack here, on which are stretched beautiful cream sheets of caul fat, from the stomachs of the cows. These will be wrapped around joints intended for roasting.

In a metal trough sit the grey intestines of a single cow, which will be thrown away.

We pass underneath the man on the scaffold, and through the line of hanging bodies waiting to be skinned and legged, up a little step that is slippery with blood. Then we walk outside, to where the cattle are waiting between their rails, and climb up some steps to look down into the shooting box, which is a deep concrete trough. Tadhg, the man who kills the cows, stands on the platform next to us. He stuns them by sending a bolt through their skulls.

Stephen shows me the captive bolt gun, which doesn't look like a gun at all – more like a power drill. It is inspected and serviced regularly. The external humane officer, Stephen says, is 'lethal', by which he means she's good at her job. 'I think she's a vegetarian.'

There are 35,000 to 40,000 cattle killed in Ireland every week. Which, as Stephen says, is 'a quare amount of cattle'.

Tadhg is a beefy man, tall and fair and ruddy-faced, wearing his uniform shirt, which is red. He is a farmer himself. He starts to drive the black and white Hereford cross into the shooting box. In the big factories, there are restraints in the shooting boxes, which, according to Stephen, cause the animals stress and darken the beef. There are no restraints in the shooting box here. 'We bring them in nice and calm,' he says.

'Nice and calm' is, evidently, a relative state. The cow, which has up to now been silent, starts skittering and reversing: she does not want to go forward into the box. ('Cows are always apprehensive about any change to their environment,' a vet will tell me later.) Then she is there, her sides up tight to the walls of the box. And Tadhg is above her with the gun, and there is a loud dull bang. Whether the bang is due to the sound of the captive bolt entering her captive skull or whether it is the sound of the door of the enclosure opening onto the other side is impossible to say.

As the cow is hoisted out of the box, her legs are kicking. 'That's just nerves,' says Stephen. 'She's dead. Look at her eye.'

It's true: the eye is steady. But she is not dead yet. The captive bolt renders the animal unconscious. And now an electrical stimulator is being sent through her, to hasten the draining of blood from the carcass. It also causes her to twitch. Tadhg, looking bigger than ever, cuts her jugular vein and carotid artery, and blood comes out of her in a gushing stream. This is what kills her.

Outside again, the little Charolais is now alone between the rails. I remark that it is hard to be the last one, and Stephen agrees. She is right back against the perimeter barrier, as if there were twenty cows in front of her; as far away from the shooting box as she can get. Silent, wide-eyed. Tadhg drives her towards the shooting box. She resists. When she is finally in it, she lies down. We'll leave her for ten or fifteen minutes, says Stephen. From the other side, you can see her hooves folded under her as she lies there. How does she know to lie down?

After a few minutes I go outside again and Tadhg is poking her with what must be a switch. I tell him not to hurry on my account. Her hooves are still folded under her.

Stephen and I go to the boning room, which is full of sheep carcasses. There were sixty or seventy killed here yesterday. Each carcass is tagged with the name of the farmer who reared it. Stephen has men who go out to the farmers. His abattoir pays slightly better than the big factories, and this means that the best of any herd comes here.

Outside, the little Charolais is now standing in the shooting box.

There is another dull bang. She is out the other side, her head on the ground, her foot already being hoisted and her eye rolled back in her head.

The electrical stimulator is attached to her. Her throat is cut and a brook of black blood is gushing out of her.

It's not the death that is hard to see; it is the life before it.

She was about eighteen months old. Some beef cows at this age are selected for breeding; the rest go to the abattoir. 'We don't like killing over thirty months,' says Stephen. The big factories will kill animals of any age, but the meat from older animals would be like 'eating the boots that you're wearing'.

The carcass of the Charolais is moving away from us now towards the skinning platform, hanging from the overhead rail by a single hoof.

Stephen says: 'I'm a Catholic born and bred and I go to Mass every week. I hope I'm going to someplace after, and that they do too.'

As a meat eater, I am morally impotent in an abattoir. The idea of dairy calves being taken from their mothers after just one day, or the thought of the conditions in which chickens are reared, upsets me as much as or even more than animal deaths. But I still feel that the deaths of the Hereford and the little Charolais were tiny tragedies, mainly because I'm not convinced that they were necessary. They died because I'm just too lazy to think of eating something else. I suspect, too, that in the context of the modern meat industry, what I am seeing at this family abattoir is the animal equivalent of witnessing George V being killed by the administration of morphine.

We go to look at the wound in the Charolais's head, amongst the tight curl of her hair. It is neat, and about three quarters of a centimetre in diameter.

There are four black and white heads hanging nearby, and greyish lungs. Stephen shows me the bavette steaks that are attached to them.

The heads must go to the incinerator – this has been the rule since the BSE outbreak in the UK in the 1990s – and the lungs will be inspected by the vet for tuberculosis and other diseases and then disposed of.

When Stephen was thinking of entering the business, he says, 'My father said to me, "If you don't do it, someone else will."'

I'm out the door at 9.58, having seen two deaths in under an hour.

6

Reuf Hrnic

3 December 2018

The graveyard at Newcastle, in west County Dublin, is on top of a slope. There are a lot of cars here, perhaps twenty, and one taxi. All belong to the funeral party. There are no women present, except me. Dress is informal; the men look like construction workers, as if they could be digging the grave.

And this is just as well, because a Bosnian funeral is a hands-on experience. First of all, the men take the lid off the rough pine coffin, known as the *tabud*, which they have built themselves. The dead body, bound in white cloth, is taken out and laid on a wooden tray. It is the body of a tall, thin man.

The men cup their hands for the recitation of the prayers. About half of them join the responses. The winter sun is low in the sky.

A tall, strong man steps forward and addresses the group. If the dead man had ever done anything against anyone here, he asks that they now forgive him.

The body is placed on the slats of raw fresh wood that have been arranged across the grave, and five men, using straps, lower it in.

Then, amazingly, a man wearing all black – the black shirt

still has the creases of newness – is also lowered very carefully, feet first, into the grave. Other men hold him by his arms, and he braces his feet and his legs into the walls of the narrow grave, essentially straddling the corpse but not touching it. Slats are then handed to him – I count nine – which he places diagonally over the corpse, working quickly. When he is finished, he raises his hands and the men pull him out. (Later, he will explain to me that this task fell to him because he is 'nearest of kin' to the dead man.)

About thirty-five men – mostly middle-aged, only one of them young – come forward one at a time to take a turn with the big shovel, tossing earth into the grave until another man steps forward from the crowd and taps him on the shoulder, indicating that it is now his turn.

Someone lights a cigarette. The roar of traffic from the N7 motorway nearby continues throughout.

The man in the new black shirt is still throwing clay into the grave when a mechanical digger, driven by an employee of the county council, starts to help filling it in. The digger is working at the head of the grave and the men are working at the foot. The body is protected from the impact of the falling earth by the slats.

The driver of the digger asks the man in the new black shirt: 'Do you want it level?' He gestures a flat surface with his hand.

The man in the black shirt nods that he does want it level.

When the digger has finished its work, the man in the new black shirt re-emerges from the crowd. He and two other men, each of them with a shovel, finish off the grave.

The driver of the mechanical digger tells me that you never have to fill in a Bosnian grave on your own. He looks at the men, who have worked so hard. 'That'd be some job when it rains,' he says.

It is important to Muslims that they are buried facing towards Mecca.

'Sure the world is round,' says the digger driver philosophically. 'Whatever way you're facing, you're facing Mecca.'

The men gather around the finished grave. A slim, dark man, the imam from the South Circular Road mosque, reads the words of a prayer from his mobile phone. The men hold their hands out, palms up, as they pray. The big man who spoke at the beginning of the burial blows his nose and wipes it. There is no sound except the roar of the traffic.

A Bosnian community became established in Ireland during the Yugoslav war of the 1990s, and many of them speak perfect Dublin. Suljo Zukanovic, who kindly drove me here today from the mosque, is one such man, now a driver for Dublin Bus. There are about 1,500 Bosnians in the city. 'Bosnians mostly live in Blanchardstown. I'd say sixty per cent live in the Blanch.'

The dead man, Reuf Hrnic, lived in Blanchardstown and died in Blanchardstown Hospital. Suljo, who did not know Reuf well, learned of his death on Facebook. He last saw him 'less than a couple of years ago in a hospital in Blanch. He had an appointment for diabetes.'

Then Reuf lost a lot of weight.

'But he was still kind of heavy. This man was a big man. I

don't think he ever worked. I think he was on the dole. He had the disabled. He used to be the goalkeeper for us. We played in Harristown Park every Saturday and Sunday.' Reuf, who was born in 1953 and who came to Ireland around 1999, often talked about going back to Banja Luka, where his mother still lived. 'He wasn't working, he couldn't help her too much,' remembers his friend Mehmet Slavotic. When his mother died, Reuf was desolate. He was unmarried, without children, did not speak English and did not have many friends amongst the Bosnian community in Dublin. His only relatives in Ireland were an aunt, with whom he lived in Mulhuddart and who died some years ago, and a cousin, who was in poor health.

Reuf was a regular customer at Mehmet's butcher's business, then located in Thomas Street. They would go for coffee together. As far as Mehmet knows, Reuf was a driver in Bosnia before the war. He shows me a photo of Reuf's Irish driving licence; and looking at that formal photo, Reuf's broad face and moustache are suddenly here and now. 'He was a beautiful man, I'm telling you,' Mehmet says. 'He would help you. When I'm talking about my friend, I am very emotional.'

Mehmet went to see Reuf in hospital several times, the final time just one week before his death. Reuf died on a Friday and was buried on a Monday. Mehmet says the rule about Muslims burying people as fast as possible is not applied so strictly in colder climates. Even in Bosnia, people who die on a Saturday are not buried until Monday, he says.

Most Bosnian Muslims were not religious before the civil war in the old Yugoslavia, Suljo tells me: it was the persecution inflicted upon them that ignited their faith. 'After the war, people started praying and believing.' But the men here today seem a relaxed and secular bunch.

Suljo's father was one of the 8,000 Bosnian Muslim men and boys who were murdered by the Bosnian Serb army at Srebrenica in 1995. 'He was shot, we think, on the twelfth of July. My mother died when I was small. I had a stepmother and they pulled my father from her on the evening of the eleventh of July. He was found in a mass grave. His foot was missing. They never found his foot.'

Suljo was in his early twenties at the time. His father, who was a policeman in the reserves, had been in the Yugoslav Communist Party as a young man. 'You had to be if you wanted to get on in life,' says Suljo. His father had encouraged his five sons to get out of Bosnia, and as a result, only Suljo was in Bosnia — there to visit his girlfriend — when the killing started. On the whole, he feels pretty lucky. 'Only my father from my house was killed. And four of my second cousins. And my sister's husband was killed. He had a problem with his leg; he was never in the army.'

His wife, as a young girl, had been in the Potočari refugee camp near Srebrenica. The Serbs separated the women from the men and boys over the age of twelve. Her father was shot. She arrived in Ireland at the age of fifteen to live with her uncle and aunt, who had already settled here. She and Suljo now have four children. They try to go back to Bosnia every July for the anniversary of the massacre.

'It's scary to look at eighty thousand graves – all white, honest to God. You can't believe it happened.'

His wife does not go to Srebrenica for the commemoration. 'She does not watch TV that day. She can't.'

Reuf Hrnic
1953–2018

7

Heroes

When Cúchulainn, the warrior demigod of Irish legend, was dying, he lashed himself to a standing stone: with his intestines, or with the breastplate of his battle armour. (The myth has come down to us with a number of interesting variations.) He did not want to die on the ground like an animal. He watched crows or perhaps a raven stumble over his intestines, which had fallen out of his body and were lying at his feet, and he laughed. He raised his sword to the heavens. He took several days to die. Or he died quickly and it was simply that the army of his enemies was too frightened to approach his body for three days. They knew that he was finally dead when they could take the sword from his hand. Or they knew he was finally dead when a raven landed on his shoulder. His enemy, Lugaid, who had killed him, came forward to claim Cúchulainn's head and the sword. But Cúchulainn's hand would not release the sword. So Lugaid cut the tendons in the dead man's arm, and when they were loosened, the falling sword cut off Lugaid's hand. Or his arm. Lugaid was killed shortly afterwards, by Cúchulainn's ally, Conall the Victorious. Lugaid asked that Conall fight him with just one hand, as Lugaid himself now only had one hand. Conall agreed, and killed Lugaid with one arm tied to his side with rope. Years before, Conall and Cúchulainn had sworn to avenge each other's deaths. Conall had told Cúchulainn, 'Thy blood shall not be cold on the earth when I avenge thee.'

Jordan Davis

On the morning of Jordan Davis's funeral, a group of six very young boys, aged between eleven and perhaps four-teen, their tummies still showing the roundness of childhood, stood outside the Church of Our Lady Immaculate in Darn-dale, dressed in their best and not knowing quite where to put themselves. The horse-drawn hearse was empty now because the coffin had gone in.

Many hearts have been broken in Darndale, including those of anyone who is interested in the possibilities of social housing. Dublin has a number of poorly designed and chron-ically neglected working-class suburbs, but the bleakness of Darndale is distinctive.

It was built in the 1970s as part of Dublin Corporation's push to get the poor out of the inner city. It followed what is known as the Radburn concept, which was conceived in America as a sort of variant of the British garden suburb idea. (In the last moments of his life, Jordan Davis ran towards Marigold Road, where he died; but he could have died in Tulip Court, or Primrose Grove, or Snowdrop Walk, without leaving Darndale.) The distinctive feature of a Radburn-style estate is that the backs of the houses, and their gardens, face the road; the front doors face on to communal laneways. The Radburn concept was adopted all over the Anglophone world, and in some places it worked well: the Village Green, in Los Angeles, has been designated a National Historic Landmark. In other places, Radburn-style estates have been disastrous failures.

The peculiar layout of Radburn estates has sometimes been seen as facilitating crime; but in Darndale, the planning errors and the culture of neglect run deeper. When I asked an architect to describe the siting of Darndale, he said, 'Plonked in a field.' Here, as elsewhere in Dublin, people were moved from crowded inner-city housing to new estates located on what had been farmland, thereby losing the intimacy and resources of urban life without gaining the amenities of a well-planned suburb. Pressed further, the architect used the term 'mono-class': no effort was made to avoid creating what was effectively a segregated ghetto for the poor. Darndale has frequently been cited, even by the Irish government, as the most deprived area in the country.

On my way here, I stopped an old man to ask directions to the church. He was pushing a bicycle loaded with what looked like fishing rods. 'It's a sad day,' he said. 'And they got his mate as well.' Seventeen hours before Jordan Davis was murdered, his friend, Sean Little, was found shot dead beside his blazing car.

I parked my car under direction from two middle-aged men, then walked down an alleyway that contained a make-shift shrine to Jordan Davis, draped with a scarf from Darndale Football Club and stacked with flowers. Jordan was shot four times while pushing his infant son in his buggy.

He was a twenty-two-year-old drug dealer, and it is believed that he was killed because he owed bigger drug dealers €70,000. It is said that when he saw the gunman coming for him, he handed his baby son to another man and ran, pursued by the gunman on a red bicycle.

The church of Our Lady Immaculate dates from the time, after Vatican II, when the Catholic Church was flirting with democracy. The altar is low, only a couple of steps above the worshippers.

In his sermon, Father Leo Philomin said that drugs make nothing but corpses. He said that Jordan Davis was not a hard man, but an insecure person whose life was terrible. A buggy, presumably containing Jordan's son, stood right beside the coffin.

In the front bench on the left-hand side sat eight slim young men with identical haircuts, leaning forward with their shoulders hunched, in the traditional posture of Irish men in church. A posture that goes back decades, if not centuries. A posture that says, 'I've turned up, I'm doing the right thing, but don't expect me to be enthusiastic.' One of them wore a baseball cap. While the young men in the front row exchanged the sign of peace by hugging each other, Father Leo stepped down from the low altar to ask the man in the baseball cap to remove it. He did.

A friend of Jordan's mother read a poem about Jordan in which she referred to him as 'my gentle giant' and talked about him 'laughing and rapping, shopping and happy'. There was warm applause.

At the end of the Mass, a young man at a computer

projected a rolling montage of photos onto a screen. Jordan as a beautiful toddler. Jordan with his younger sister, Jade, who died as a child, and then the adult Jordan at her grave. Jordan in his Dolce & Gabbana T-shirt and his Kenzo Paris T-shirt, and in his Calvin Klein sweatshirt, holding his new baby.

Outside stood two Bentley limousines and the horse-drawn hearse. The wreaths were stacked in a motor hearse. One of them was a huge facsimile of a Rolex watch, with a real clock ticking at the centre of it.

'Tomorrow's the big one,' said one of the undertakers. He was referring to the funeral of Jordan Davis's friend Sean Little. 'That one is twelve thousand and this one was four thousand.'

Outside in the alleyway, the door of the community centre, attached to the church and called the New Life Centre, was locked when I tried it. The woman who seemed to be in charge let me in to use the Ladies, then shut the front door behind me. When I emerged, a very thin young man wearing shorts and his jumper pulled up to mask his face, and with his hand down his shorts in what I took to be a mimicry of masturbation, said, 'Are you the reporter?' His friend offered me a joint, which I declined.

Sean Little

The undertaker was right about Sean Little's funeral. It was much bigger.

In Kilmore West – not far from Darndale, or from Coolock, where Sean Little lived – I left my car in Eagle Park and passed Tranquillity Grove as I walked.

In the car park of the church of St Luke the Evangelist, forty minutes before the funeral started, two glamorous young women, one blonde and one brunette, sat in a huge white jeep. A young teenager in a pale grey tracksuit looked wretched waiting outside the church with his phone. How miserable to be the first of your friends to arrive.

No one here seemed to have heard, or to have paid attention to, the statement earlier in the week from the Archbishop of Dublin about 'show funerals' for people involved in crime. He seemed to be saying that the archdiocese would not continue to allow its churches to be used for such funerals.

Five Mercedes stretch limousines were parked outside the church as we waited for the cortège to arrive on foot: this felt like a show of strength. We watched as enormous floral tributes were carried into the church: 'Bro', 'Grandson' and so on, but also a huge arch made of white chrysanthemums, and two large pictures – one of a mountain against a blue sky and the other a portrait of Sean himself – made entirely of flowers.

The coffin arrived, preceded by a piper and followed by a large crowd. The bare legs of the young women flashed in the sun as the cortège approached. There were a lot of gardaí on the road. Inside, the church was packed, with some girls coming in late. It takes a long time to put the cocktail look together, and it is no easy task at this hour of the morning: satin skirts, square-necked tops with transparent panels, hair bands, deep tans, black jumpsuits and over-the-knee boots.

Beside the altar stood several of the floral displays. The mountain scene was framed entirely with red chrysanthemums and must have been more than four feet high.

A friend of Sean's, handsome in a white shirt that could have been made of damask, approached the altar high-shouldered, head down, as if he was about to take a penalty he was pretty confident of scoring. He told us that Sean was a fitness fanatic. He was the funniest, lovingest, most caring friend. 'Sean,' said Brandon from the altar, 'I love you. I can't wait to see you again.'

The newspapers have speculated that Sean Little – who, like Jordan Davis, died at the age of twenty-two – was lured to his death by someone he knew, and that he died because the so-called 'Gucci gang' in Finglas owed him about €200,000; that it was therefore simply cheaper and easier to kill him. The Gucci gang is said to be a subset of the Kinahan gang.

On the way out, the piper played 'Dark Isle', 'Abide with Me', 'Going Home' and 'Amazing Grace'.

During the fortnight between the deaths of Sean Little and Jordan Davis and their funerals, when their bodies were with the coroner, a man was murdered by three masked men in the driveway of the house in Kilbarron Avenue where the Little family were said to be holding a wake for Sean. The security cameras on the house were said to have been turned to the wall about an hour before the shooting. Hamid Sanambar, an Iranian in his forties, was suspected by Little's associates of having had him killed. It is thought he had gone to the house to pay his respects and to deny having had any part in the murder. A year later, gardaí told reporters that Sanambar had probably had nothing to with it.

Four days after Sean Little's funeral, in the Fingal graveyard where both he and Jordan Davis are buried, it is raining, and it takes quite a while to find their graves. The huge watch lies on Jordan's grave, in pride of place among the other wreaths. There is a bottle of Ribena, four plastic-wrapped bouquets and a can of Coke at the top left-hand side of the plot. Three young people have just left.

Sean Little's grave is situated near the wall that separates the graveyard from the Malahide Road. It's not far from where he was found beside his burning car. There are nine wreaths here: 'Brother', 'Nephew', 'Son', 'Cuz', 'Godson', 'Grandson', 'Our Sean', 'Jumbo' and an arrangement in the shape of the cross. Potted chrysanthemums. Yellow roses. Bunches of flowers in cellophane. The big flower picture is here too, its sky made of chrysanthemums dyed blue. But its green countryside has faded, or perhaps been pilfered for souvenirs. A lone succulent is all that is left of that constructed Irish countryside.

In the graveyard I meet a man tending the immaculate grave of his nine-year-old daughter, who died of a brain tumour. I mention Sean Little's grave. 'My brother's mother-in-law is buried here,' he says. 'They're not too happy about it.'

On my way back from the graveyard, I drop in to Clare Hall shopping centre, just across the Malahide Road from Darndale, where my stepdaughter is working. She knew the circumstances of Sean Little's murder before they had been reported because, she tells me, one of the girls she works with lived on the same road as him. After that murder and the murder of Jordan Davis, there were helicopters overhead and cops everywhere, and she saw them on her way to work.

There is no such place as 'gangland'. These dramas played out between pathetic men take place in ordinary working-class areas where ordinary people are getting on with their lives. When she was seven, my stepdaughter and her mother were in McDonald's in Donaghmede Shopping Centre when the man serving at the drive-thru hatch was stabbed in the neck with a screwdriver. They saw him moments after the attack, clutching at his neck, from which the screwdriver still protruded. That story made for an interesting weekend visit, with a seven-year-old explaining that the assailant was a junkie.

In September 2012, the criminal and republican paramilitary Alan Ryan was murdered within yards of my stepdaughter's home. 'It was about four p.m.,' she says, 'because I was just back to the house from school.'

Alan Ryan's blood was left at the site of his murder for a number of days. For the full paramilitary funeral, my stepdaughter recalls, undercover gardaí were stationed in houses in the area.

Alan Ryan's brother, Vinnie, was murdered in 2016 — 'but that was in Finglas' — as he dropped his girlfriend and the mother of his child back to her house. The car of another brother, who was not involved in crime, was set on fire outside the Ryan house. These people were and are my step-daughter's neighbours.

My stepdaughter is philosophical about all of this. 'There's violent people and then there's circumstances. When you live in an estate which is between Darndale and a new-build like Clongriffin, the average age is going to stay low. It's easier for them to congregate. And then there's nothing to do in my area whatsoever. There's not even a community centre.'

In 2014, a man called Declan Smith was shot outside a crèche in Donaghmede, and died some days later. The newspapers said that he was a dissident republican/criminal, originally from Northern Ireland. He was said to have been one of the first people to arrive on the scene of Alan Ryan's death in 2012; it is also said that Ryan had been on his way to see Smith that day. In any event, Declan Smith was shot in the face by a masked man just after dropping his child to the crèche, in front of other parents who were doing the same.

In the Coroner's Court: the Case of Declan Davitt and Martin Needham

It is a cloudy September day in Castlebar, County Mayo. The town's fine courthouse looks out onto the pleasant green area known as the Mall. There is quite a crowd of people waiting outside Court Four – all the local newspapers plus an RTÉ camera crew and the reporter Teresa Mannion.

The courtroom is modern and full of blonde benches. The jury of six – all of them older men – sit near the Mayo coroner, Patrick O'Connor. The body of the courtroom is filled with people in dark clothing, and on my side sit five gardaí and one member of the coastguard in uniform.

We are here for the inquest into the deaths of Declan Davitt and Martin Needham in Louisburgh, early on Christmas morning in 2017.

The first witness called is Thomas McGreal, a strong-looking young man with fine shoulders and a flat stomach. At the time of the accident he was only twenty, seven years younger than both Davitt and Needham. In his statement, which he chooses to have read for him by Sergeant McLoughlin, he describes how, on Christmas Eve 2017, he went drinking from about 3 p.m. with the two men in Johnny Mac's pub in Louisburgh. 'Then they left for another pub, where I had two ciders, so I was there about an hour.' After that they went back to Johnny Mac's. Martin Needham was driving. The car was an SUV, a black Ford Ranger.

They left Johnny Mac's late. 'We were going to the Ocean Lodge Hotel to meet friends,' Thomas McGreal testifies. 'Martin was drinking cider. Declan was drinking Special [Smithwicks with a Guinness head]. Once we had finished there we decided to buy three bottles of vodka, and three of 7 Up. So the three of us fell into the jeep. Declan decided to drive us to the Gibbonses' house.'

Mrs Mary Gibbons tells the court that she was at home in Roonagh with members of her family when, at about half past one in the morning, Declan, Martin and Thomas arrived. 'No one had any idea they were coming,' she says. 'They poured themselves drinks.' A glass was broken.

Mrs Gibbons was not impressed. 'I told the lads that they were welcome in the house any time, but not in that state. Declan said, "Do you know, you're right, Mary."' So the three visitors left. According to Thomas McGreal, one of Mary's sons had objected to Martin Needham driving, because he was so drunk. 'So Declan was driving and Martin was sitting in the front seat and I was in the back. Declan drove out of the driveway and hit a neighbour's wall with the tow bar of the jeep.' This happened three times, according to Mary's son Richard. The Gibbons family could hear a horn beep, and shouting and laughing. The lights of the jeep were going down towards the Carrowniskey river.

'I could see the river,' Thomas McGreal told the court. 'It was high and in full flow.'

Declan was trying to bring the jeep across the river, at a crossing point sometimes used by vehicles when the river is low. The wheels of the jeep spun. He reversed and tried again. The next thing Thomas knew was that the front part of the jeep was in the river and the interior was filling up with water.

At first, Thomas McGreal said, 'The lads were starting to laugh and thinking it was great crack.' But as the car filled with water, Declan and Martin began to panic.

Thomas testified that he got out of the SUV through a window and swam ashore. 'I could hear screaming from the jeep. Then silence. I think I walked into an electric fence. I then started to run up to Gibbons's — some of the family were still up. They called 999 and gave me blankets and told me to stay where I was.'

The fourth witness is Nora O'Malley, the girlfriend of Richard Gibbons, a slim young woman with red hair and glasses, wearing a close-fitting jacket in pale grey, black leggings and high black boots. She was in the Gibbons house on the night of Christmas Eve, she says. She testifies that after Thomas arrived back at the house, she rang 999. There was some difficulty getting a phone working, and she had to use Richard's phone.

Witness five is Richard Gibbons, with tight-cropped reddish hair, a young man who looks like an athlete. He is wearing a grey jumper and jeans.

After Thomas McGreal raised the alarm, Richard left the house and 'checked where the road entered the river but there was no sign of the jeep. I searched the fields as well but there was no sign of the jeep.'

The bodies were found at about 4 p.m. on Christmas Day, after a search in pouring rain. They were found downstream, in Roonith lake, where the Carrowniskey river enters the Atlantic. A coastguard officer found them at approximately three or four fathoms: under eighteen to twenty-four feet of water.

Witness nine is Sergeant Ciaran Diffley, a trim man with grey hair, slightly tanned. It fell to him to inform the Davitt and Needham families of the disaster that night.

In response to a question from the coroner, Sergeant Diffley says: 'At the scene itself I would describe both radio and phone coverage as non-existent.'

Witness eleven is Sergeant Gabriel McLoughlin, of the forensic investigation team. He shows the court twenty-eight photographs of the scene, taken by a colleague. One of them is of what he calls the 'road' leading to the informal river crossing. It is, on the evidence of the photo, more like a track, and Sergeant McLoughlin says it is about two metres wide. He testifies that the river was 'twelve metres wide and two metres deep'.

The solicitor for the Needham family asks: 'Were there any road signs or anything?'

Garda Gabriel McLoughlin: 'No, absolutely none.'

Solicitor: 'Any road markings?'

Garda Gabriel McLoughlin: 'No.'

The Ford Ranger, Sergeant McLoughlin says, was found 175 metres downriver of where it entered the river.

Dr Fadel Bennani is a consultant pathologist at University Hospital in Castlebar. He is very handsome, with white hair.

On 26 December he performed an autopsy on Mr Declan Davitt, date of birth 19 August 1990, and Mr Martin Needham, date of birth 15 March 1990.

He found a lot of frothy secretions from the nose and mouth on both men – an indication of drowning. Both were in good health and otherwise uninjured. The cause of death for both men, he says, was 'asphyxia by drowning'.

As is routine, he sent blood samples for toxicology testing. Declan Davitt's blood-alcohol level was 260 milligrams per 100 millilitres of blood.

Coroner: 'That's quite high. What is the legal limit for driving?'

Dr Bennani: 'Eighty.'

In other words, Declan Davitt was more than three times

over the legal limit when he died. And he was driving only because he was perceived to be less drunk than Martin Needham. (That perception was correct: Martin Needham's blood-alcohol level was 334.)

Dr Bennani is the last witness. After his testimony is complete, the coroner tells the jury that the purpose of an inquest is to discover the reason the persons died; to establish where they lived; and to establish where they died. He says there are a number of verdicts open to the jury: accidental death ('that is, a case of pure accident with no participation in the accident or part in causing it'); misadventure ('an accident with a certain amount of intent'); or an open verdict ('where you cannot be certain with regard to the other verdicts').

The verdict given by the jury is one of accidental death.

After noting this verdict, the coroner says: 'It remains for me to say that sudden death at any time is the most difficult and most trying event. But at Christmas time it is devastating not just for the family but for the community and for the entire county. I would also like to commend Thomas McGreal, whose forthright evidence was most helpful. And to extend the thanks of the whole community to Sergeant Diffley: he had the difficult task of telling both the Needham and the Davitt families the news of the deaths. All the gardaí, who worked in particularly difficult climatic conditions. I do hope the families get some consolation from the lives they had, and also the crack they had.'

The coroner also says that he is 'very concerned at the lack of telecom coverage' in the vicinity of the disaster. 'A lot of people live there and they deserve the full facilities.'

And so we stumble out into the sunny autumn day, a bit stunned by the detail of what we have heard, and yet perhaps not greatly the wiser. I notice the blank faces of the families, who must be relieved that inquest day is over. I notice the light in the eyes of the reporters, who are running towards their deadlines. We all know that this is a great story and a terrible story – a sensation.

The coroner chose to highlight the patchy phone coverage in the area, which seems to have made it harder for Nora O'Malley to raise the alarm, and to have hindered the gardaí as well. He did not choose to highlight the fact that there was a road that crossed the bed of the Carrowniskey river and that there was no sign or barrier preventing vehicles from using this crossing.

And then there is the other river: the river of alcohol that runs through the deaths of young males in cars on Irish country roads. This did not get a mention in the coroner's concluding remarks. The jury, for its part, concluded that getting into a vehicle after some eleven hours' heavy drinking, and attempting to drive across a river visibly in spate, did not constitute misadventure: it was merely an accident, involving, per the coroner's instructions, 'no participation in the accident or part in causing it'.

What is the purpose of a coroner's inquest? This is a murky area, and it is complicated by a growing sense that Ireland's coronial service is not fit for purpose. In 2000, a Department of Justice working group identified a need for 'radical reform' of the service, but this never happened. (Legislation amending the 1962 Coroners Act would be enacted in 2019, the year after the Davitt/Needham inquest, but its effects were modest, and an April 2021 report by the Irish Council for Civil Liberties would speak of 'a network of part-time coroners without the necessary support of specialist, trained investigators and dedicated administrative staff'.)

Some inquests have a galvanizing effect. In 2013, an inquest reached a verdict of medical misadventure in the death of Savita Halappanavar, who developed sepsis in pregnancy and died of cardiac arrest because the staff of an Irish hospital declined to abort a foetus that had no hope of surviving, believing they were not allowed to do so under the law. Writing about the inquest in the *Irish Times*, Ruadhán Mac Cormaic noted that there is no broad agreement as to the purpose of an inquest. Some believe its role is essentially to rubber-stamp the findings of the post-mortem examination. Others believe it serves – or ought to serve – a broader social function. The Halappanavar case, Mac Cormaic wrote, demonstrated that 'a well-run inquest . . . can help society to learn lessons'.

According to an analysis by the Road Safety Authority of coronial files on deaths between 2013 and 2017, more than a third of people who died on Irish roads had alcohol in their systems. Sixty-two per cent of those who died with alcohol in their systems were the drivers in the fatal collisions; ninety-two per cent were male; and more than four fifths were under the age of forty-five.

Walking out of the courtroom following the inquest into the deaths of Declan Davitt and Martin Needham, it was hard to feel confident that anything had been learned. Perhaps the problem of young men driving cars while drunk is so pervasive that we have come to view it as a force of nature: a force as unstoppable as the flow of the Carrowniskey river on Christmas Eve 2017.

In the Coroner's Court: the Case of Joseph Kierans Regan

The coroner's court in Castlebar is much quieter the following day, when the inquest of Joseph Kierans Regan is called. Both parents of this dead young man are present in court.

Garda Brosnan tells the court that he is stationed in Castlebar. On the morning of 16 February 2018, he was called to the Woodview B&B at Breaffy, just outside the town, where there had been a sudden death. At 7.45 a.m., he found a man unresponsive in bed. Death was pronounced at 8.45. At 4.58 that afternoon, the deceased man's father, Joe Kierans, formally identified the body.

The second witness is a very young man called Brendan Halliday. He gave a statement to the gardaí on the day Joseph Kierans Regan's death was pronounced. It said that he worked as a fitter and was a colleague of Joseph Kierans Regan, with whom he had worked for two or three months and whom he called Joe.

'Yesterday myself and Joe were working in Cork. Then we drove to Limerick, where we had another job. Then to Castlebar.'

In Castlebar, Joseph and Brendan met another young man,

Jamie Reilly. 'At about nine p.m. Joe and Jamie and me drove into Castlebar. We went into the Bungalow Bar and played pool for forty-five minutes to an hour. I reckon Joe only had two or three pints in the pub. He mentioned he was tired.'

Back at the bed and breakfast where they were staying, Joseph and Brendan were sharing a room.

'The last thing he said was "Night, lad."'

On the subject of Joseph's drug use, Brendan Halliday told gardaí: 'I don't know if he smoked weed every day. I did know he took tablets every day. Prescription tablets.'

The next morning, when he woke in the room in the B&B that he was sharing with Joseph, Brendan noticed 'a lot of black liquid' on the sheets of Joseph's bed.

Jamie Reilly takes the stand: another very young man. He had been working in Castlebar installing shutter doors. He too chooses to have his statement read out by a guard.

Jamie thought Joe had had only one pint in the Bungalow Bar, not the two or three that Brendan recalled. Like Brendan, he remembered Joseph saying he was 'very tired'.

After he learned of Joseph's death, Jamie says, 'I rang my boss, Matt Duffy. I'm only with this company seven months. I got on well with Joe. He never missed a day of work.'

It is a sad tribute.

Now a garda takes the stand. He testifies that Joseph Regan was found lying face down, with blood visible around his nose and mouth. He says, 'I recovered the following items. A syringe and a spoon in the tracksuit pockets. A cannabis grinder. Two Xanax tablets. Also three hundred euros in a wash bag.'

Joseph's mother, Maggie Regan, is crying now.

The pathologist, Dr Fadel Bennani, takes the stand. He performed a full post-mortem on Joseph Regan on the day of his death. 'There were multiple needle marks in both arms and legs. The heart was normal. The brain was normal . . . There was some congestion on the lungs.'

Dr Bennani sent some samples to the laboratory for analysis. The results were positive for morphine and for a by-product of heroin: the level of a borderline overdose, he says. The presence of alcohol was 'very mild. But this combination of substances . . .' He explains to the family that alcohol exacerbates the effect of heroin.

'Heroin, was it?' asks Joe's father.

'Yes,' says Dr Bennani.

'Overdose?' asks Joseph's mother.

The coroner nods.

Dr Bennani found no disease present in Joseph. 'He is a healthy chap,' he says with a smile.

Joseph's mother throws her beautiful eyes up to heaven.

The coroner finds that Joseph's death was caused by acute respiratory depression due to heroin intoxication. He died one month to the day before his twenty-ninth birthday.

Joseph's former colleagues Brendan and Jamie leave the courtroom together, their heads down in misery. The true cause of his death seems to have come as a shock to them. They had spoken in praise of him. They seem to have loved him.

When I meet her nine months later, Joseph's mother tells me that his death was not a shock to her. We are sitting in her cosy living room in County Cavan, with a wood fire burning in the grate. Maggie is carefully made up, prettier than ever.

Like many people who have been bereaved in the most savage of ways, she is willing to talk pretty frankly. Her son's death 'was something I never wanted to happen, but it was something I expected'.

She believes his overdose was not an accident: she thinks he committed suicide. 'He had a lot of things hanging over him. He had a suspended sentence and it was up the week after he died.'

Between the police, the gangsters, the neighbours who shouted abuse at Joseph in the street and the prison sentence, it was easy to see that he had a lot to escape. 'The pathologist told me that he even had needle marks in his toes.'

This was not a future that Maggie had anticipated for her son when he was little, though she always had concerns about him.

'He was always quiet,' she says. 'When he was a little boy he used to chat to me, but with other people he was very quiet. He'd sit in his room and read books – I still have some of his Enid Blyton books in there – and I thought, that's not right.' His younger brother, she says, 'mixed with other kids much more'.

When Joseph was in his final year of his primary education, the family moved house. He was now a town boy in a country school – the same school Maggie herself had attended – and he was badly bullied. 'He was very, very tall, and stick thin and paranoid about his weight. I went into the school, to the same master who had taught me, to talk about the bullying. Joseph would stand by the gate pillar of the school sobbing, and beg me not to make him go in.'

It was at secondary school in a nearby town that he first took drugs. Maggie learned that from reading the journal he later kept during his time in rehab, which described his history of drug use. 'He started on drugs at twelve years of age, on cocaine and hash. Cocaine – I didn't know what it was.'

After three years, he moved to a different secondary school, mainly because his younger brother had started there.

'The thing is that he was very intelligent and he got great school reports. His Leaving Cert was very good – I don't know how he did it. He was doing acid and everything. Even I know now what acid is. I said to [her then husband] Joe, "Imagine what he could have done if he tried."

'He had a great head. And great hands. He knew immediately how things worked.'

When he was twenty, Joseph was arrested at a house in Bailieborough with a bag of Ecstasy tablets. He was convicted and sentenced to four months in prison, with two months suspended.

'When he got out one Sunday, this is back when I used to buy the papers, there were big headlines about the Dundon and McCarthy drug gangs in Dublin, and there were photos. I remember Joseph pointing out a gang member to me and saying, "He looked after me in prison." I didn't want to think about what that had involved.'

According to Maggie, it was while he was in prison that

Joseph started using heroin, although she didn't realize that at the time.

Shortly after his release, she heard him on the phone, arguing with someone. This was out of character for him. He told her he was arguing with a friend of his, but Maggie knew that wasn't true.

'It was a Tuesday morning. I was washing the dishes in the sink. Joseph came and stood by me. He was as white as a ghost. He stood there and he said, "I'm in trouble." I said, "What kind of trouble? What are you talking about?" He said, "They're after me, that gang in Dublin."'

He said the Dublin gang was looking for €10,000, arising from the Ecstasy tablets he'd been caught with and another batch that he had buried and lost.

That morning, Maggie and Joseph ran through their options, and they were few. 'We'd no money. We'd nothing to sell. This is a council house – it's rented.'

The gang had already made Joseph show them where he and his family lived.

Eventually it was decided that he would have to leave the country. Maggie rang her sister, who lived in the UK. By Thursday, Joseph was on his way to England. 'We got him on the boat. He'd no passport, no nothing. He got very sick in England – he'd been on heroin and I didn't know.'

In England, he was put on methadone, and he got a job on the site of the London Olympics. But in March 2011, he came home, broke.

In 2012, he entered rehab at Cuan Mhuire in Athy, County Kildare. It was here he kept the journal that Maggie subsequently read. When he left, however, he was straight back into the grip of the local gangs. He was driven to the house of three old bachelors who lived together on their farm. Maggie had known them since her youth. Joseph pushed the door in, but the old man said he had no money. Joseph panicked and cut himself on his hand before he fled on foot, dropping his mobile phone on the way.

'I was coming home to watch *Emmerdale*, so it was seven o'clock in the evening. On my way home I passed the house where the three old men lived and I saw the ambulance. I thought one of them had been taken ill. When I got home, Joseph asked if he could have the car. I didn't notice the cut on his hand.'

She lent him her car very reluctantly – he did not have either a licence or insurance. While she was watching *Emmerdale*, two detectives arrived at the house looking for Joseph. They told Maggie what had happened.

After the detectives had left, Joseph came home. Maggie told him what the detectives had said, and he immediately confessed to her, saying that he had been driven to the old men's house by the man who acted as the debt collector for the Dublin drug gangs.

'After that, he couldn't walk up the town,' Maggie says. 'Nobody liked him because of robbing the old man. Seemingly there was a petition to get rid of him out of the housing estate. People shouted abuse at him in the street.'

Joseph stopped going out for a while, but one night he ventured out with his girlfriend. They met two young men, who invited them to go with them to a party in another town. They took the bus to the town, where the two men 'beat the crap out of' Joseph. Eventually Joseph's brother found him, unconscious, across from the church in Cootehill.

In 2013, Maggie says, three men turned up at the house where Joseph and his girlfriend were living. Joseph refused to come out and talk to them, and closed the door. They shot through the door, and hit him in the foot. He told Maggie that he believed the man who shot him was a local debt collector, and that he was trying to kneecap him.

In his work as a fitter installing doors, Maggie says, 'He was getting five hundred euros clear a week.' But he was borrowing money from her every week – money she didn't really have.

By this stage Joseph and his girlfriend had a little boy, but in the October before he died, he came back to live with his mother, siblings and stepfather in their little house. He slept on the couch on which I am now sitting, because there was no bed for him at the time.

One weekend, Maggie and her partner returned to the house and found Joseph 'off his face' and holding a bag.

Maggie grabbed the bag from him. 'And inside there's saline water and then there's a spoon and a wee brown bottle with white powder.'

Since Joseph's death, Maggie has been tortured by all the things she doesn't know about his life. 'You don't know what he may have done to keep up his habit. I'll never get the answers.' These are the things she thinks about in her grief.

Strange things bring him back to her. 'Just a smell or a colour.'

The pathologist at the inquest left her in no doubt about how much heroin he had been taking around the time of his death. 'He had no veins left.'

She thought she would be less worried after Joseph died, but this has not proved to be the case. She is anxious that the gangs might still try to collect their money from other members of the family.

Three years on, Maggie is in her second year of training as a youth worker. Her grandson, now nearly six, has been living with her for the past year. The drug gangs are active in Cavan still.

Bragan Bog, County Monaghan, 28 September 2018

No one wants to go to the high lonesome bogland of north Monaghan first thing in the morning. But here we are, driving out of Monaghan town on the Scotstown road. Past the sign for Monaghan Rugby Club. Through Tydavnet, a tiny village that was the home of St Dympna, before she fled her pagan father for what is now Belgium.

Bert is in front of me in his car. He left the neighbouring county of Cavan in 1966 and became a policeman in the UK. Now he works for the Independent Commission for the Location of Victims' Remains (ICLVR) – one week on, and then two weeks off. He drives like a policeman, precisely – and I mean precisely – on the speed limit at all times.

After about twenty-five minutes, we come to a gate. 'Only another half a mile,' says Bert as he stops to open and close it. We drive what seems like much more than half a mile over an unpaved track. The bog is a vast wide-open space – a sea of brown-black earth. Imagine being brought here to be murdered. In November.

My phone pings with a message from the UK mobile phone network: we are that close to the border.

This is a high place. It is blasted by the wind. It is colder than where we came from. Where the road stops are four dark blue steel containers and two cabins for toilets – rather touchingly, 'Ladies' is written on one of them. The containers hold an office for Bert, a canteen, a storage space and a generator.

I have brought both wellingtons and hiking boots, I tell Bert a little proudly. He says that neither will be necessary, because I won't be walking on the bog, but standing here, not far from the blue containers and a little to the left of them.

'Sky were here and I didn't let them further than there,' he says, gesturing to the road.

The ICLVR's brief is to seek 'the location of the remains of victims of paramilitary violence ("the Disappeared") who were murdered and buried in secret arising from the conflict in Northern Ireland'. We look out onto acres of excavated bog; about twenty-one acres have been dug up in the search for the remains of Columba McVeigh. The bog has been rolled back like a huge carpet, leaving a vast area of exposed peat. It is like a scene from a science fiction film showing the agricultural practices of an alien planet. Four orange diggers and about seven human figures, also cloaked in orange, are toiling away in it like ants.

They are working on a grid system, says Bert. The orange diggers are standing on mats of steel. They are operating a relay. The ground they are shifting has been moved before, in previous searches for Columba McVeigh.

'This will be the last search,' says Bert. 'If he's here, we will find him. It's a deeper dig. We won't be taking any chances. We'll be going deeper than we've ever been before.'

Columba McVeigh grew up in the small town of Donagh-more, in County Tyrone. In 2018, his younger brother Oliver told Keith Duggan of the *Irish Times*, 'He could be a wee bit daft and wasn't always the sharpest cookie. He had a big heart. He and my mother got on like a house on fire. Very close. He'd give you the bite out of his mouth.'

Much about the life and death of Columba McVeigh remains uncertain – starting with the date of his birth. His age at the time of his abduction has been stated to be seventeen, or nineteen. But according to the ICLVR, he was born on 27 September 1955, which would have made him twenty years old in November 1975, when he disappeared.

Columba left school early and worked in a local chicken hatchery, until the IRA blew it up. His trouble began in 1974, when the family home was searched by soldiers, who said they had found bullets hidden in a cigarette box. Columba was charged with possession of the bullets, and sent on remand to Crumlin Road jail in Belfast, where he was held with Provisional IRA prisoners.

Every Saturday, Oliver and his mother Vera travelled to Belfast to visit him in prison. Columba would often be black and blue, according to Oliver. He told his mother and little brother that the prison authorities had beaten him, but Oliver told Keith Duggan he was sure it was the Provisionals who had done it.

There is a theory that Columba McVeigh's arrest was trumped-up, but we can't know that for sure. There is also a theory that the security forces intended to use him as an informer in the Provisional wing of Crumlin Road prison, or in his local area, but we don't know that for sure either. And even if this was the plan, we can't know to what extent, if at all, Columba went along with it.

When Columba McVeigh got out of prison, his parents told him to go to Dublin. This he did. On Halloween night in 1975, he was abducted.

The McVeighs had no idea what had happened to him. They thought he might be in the UK, or even in America. Years passed. Vera used to say that he would come back one day, perhaps with a car full of grandchildren. They continued to buy birthday and Christmas presents for him. They wouldn't even go on holidays in case he returned while they were away. His dog, a red setter called Dusty, used to sit waiting for him on the pavement outside their council house.

On Palm Sunday in 1999, Oliver McVeigh came back from Mass to see a strange car parked in his cul-de-sac. A local republican read a statement telling the family that Columba was dead, killed by the Provisional IRA as an informer. Oliver had been due to work that Sunday. Now he had to go and tell his mother. According to the journalist Susan McKay, who interviewed Vera several times, when her son broke the news, she said: 'The bastards didn't have the balls to tell me to my face.'

Some of her own neighbours knew what had happened to her son. But Vera McVeigh was never visited by either the gardaí or the RUC in connection with Columba's death. Nobody was looking for him.

Gradually, greater attention came to be trained on Columba and the other people abducted and killed by the IRA: the Disappeared. The Independent Commission was established in 1999, with a remit to investigate sixteen cases. In 2003, Vera McVeigh rejected the Provisionals' apology to the families of the Disappeared. What she wanted – what the families of the Disappeared generally wanted – was the body of her loved one. Anything else was a distraction.

In May 2007, Vera McVeigh died at the age of eighty-two. She was buried under the gravestone that carried the name of her husband, who had died in 1997, and also the name of her son, whose body had still not been found.

On a couple of occasions, during a previous search, Vera had been brought here to Bragan bog. It was terrible to see her in such a desolate place, her sons said.

The search that is being prepared here today will be the fifth; it was started on foot of improved information. (The commission can't share details of the information it receives, but what is involved, generally, is IRA members disclosing what they recall of the burial places of people they disappeared. In the case of Columba McVeigh, this involves memories that are well over forty years old: even with the best will in the world, this is an imprecise undertaking.)

The forestry authorities own this land now, although local people still come up to dig turf. At one time the road used to go even further into the bog. But you look at this place, the tips of blue hills in the distance, with plantations of conifers on either side of it, and the big dark excavated floor in the middle, and then you look at yourself and at Bert, and you wonder how a skeleton could ever be found in what is effectively an Irish desert.

I don't know, says Bert. A skeleton had turned up beside the A1 at Peterborough after having been missing for six years. 'He was within his clothes. Stephen Varra, I still remember his name.'

Stephen Varra was found in a drain by someone out hunting rabbits. There was flesh still attached to his thighbone. His two shoes were sticking out of the ground. He had left his home hundreds of miles away, and vanished. Nobody knew why.

At break time, everyone sings 'Happy Birthday' to Heather, one of the archaeologists. All of them are dressed in rain gear and covered in black mud, so it is impossible to tell who is an archaeologist and who is the driver of a digger.

Her best birthday ever, Heather says, was when she was on a dig at Bushmills and everyone baked something, so there were lots of cakes.

Bert says he'd better wash the floor of the cabin. As an expert avoider of washing my own floor, I wonder if it is really worth it. 'To impress Jon,' says Bert, smiling. Jon, another senior investigator with the ICLVR, is taking over from Bert next week.

I go to sit in the car, to let people have their break in peace. I sit in the luxury of draught-free warmth and watch the little birds. I remember covering the funeral of a school-girl who had been killed in a school bus crash in County Meath. The funeral was in a tiny church in the countryside in the summertime. We stood outside in the cow parsley that grew in the ditch. Her mother came walking to the church, tanned after a recent foreign holiday. When she saw her daughter's coffin, she reared back, she shied like a horse, and her legs gave way beneath her, so that she had to be sup-ported on either side. That is the strength of grief when a mother loses her child. Where does that grief go when you don't know what happened to your child, or why, or where his body is buried?

I try to remember the labours of Sisyphus, and I wonder will the workmen here ever be able to construct a memorial to the slim bones of Columba McVeigh, as they have made memorials at the site of every disappeared person whose remains they have located. The men are particularly pleased with the memorial they made to Seamus Ruddy, a member of the Irish National Liberation Army, when they finally dis-covered his remains in a forest in Pont-de-l'Arche near Rouen in 2017. They picked out the shape of a cross in the sandy soil and carefully filled it with small stones they had found on site.

The memorial to Brendan Megraw, who was found at Oristown in County Meath in October 2014, is three big stones, or small boulders, placed one on top of the other. It looks prehistoric. The memorial to Kevin McKee and Seamus Wright, found in a single grave at Coghalstown in County Meath in June 2015, is a single big stone.

The team here works from eight in the morning until five in the afternoon. Rain, mud, cold, futility.

To have the body is everything. Asking for the bodies, begging for the bodies, digging for the bodies. Don't make us look like fools when all we want is a funeral in a small town.

The fifth excavation of Bragan bog was unsuccessful, and in September 2019 the search for Columba McVeigh was finally called off. Perhaps those who murdered him can no longer remember where precisely they buried him. Perhaps his body was moved, at some stage, to another location. Perhaps it was never in Bragan bog in the first place.

Of the original sixteen cases under the remit of the Independent Commission, the remains of thirteen of the Disappeared have been located. The exceptions are Robert Nairac, a British Army officer abducted during an undercover operation in south Armagh; Joe Lynskey, a Belfast paramilitary who was disappeared during an internal IRA feud; and Columba McVeigh.

The Cliff Edge

Today – like every day in normal times – the Cliffs of Moher are swarming with tourists. There are people as far as the eye

182

can see: which is just as far as Hag's Head, about six or eight kilometres away.

In the midst of all this walks Tom Doherty, dressed in yellow and wearing dark glasses. He is employed as a ranger here. Occasionally he breaks off from our conversation to tell one of the more agile tourists to come back from the cliff edge, where they are posing for photographs. They must come down to the other side of the huge pieces of slate that stand as a type of barrier at the edge. At one point he uses a whistle to attract their attention.

The Cliffs of Moher, on the Atlantic coast in County Clare, stand two hundred metres above the Atlantic. People come here from all over Ireland, and all over the world, to enjoy the view and to take selfies. And some people come here to throw themselves off. No one has ever survived the fall.

Tom says that the death toll from suicide here in the worst year he is aware of was eight; in the average year it is five or six. 'The powers that be don't want to talk about it,' he says. 'There'd be quite a lot of casualties, that's what we say. We don't talk about it afterwards. We don't highlight it.'

As a volunteer with the local Doolin Search and Rescue, of which he is deputy officer in charge, Tom also pulls the bodies from the water.

'So far this year's been quiet,' he says. (We spoke in 2018.) 'A lot of people have been taken back from the edge. Talked back. You'd notice someone acting a bit suspicious. They'd be watching you.'

Not every death at the Cliffs of Moher is a suicide. 'We

had one of those base jumpers, he got killed last year. I think he was in his forties.'

In 2000, a group of abseilers raising money for charity descended the cliffs, only for a fall of rock to kill two of them when they had reached the bottom.

But these accidents are the exceptions. Most of the people who die here do so having chosen to end their lives, and sometimes having travelled long distances. 'One came from South Korea last year. They've come from Japan. From the States. From Germany. From Spain, from Italy. Some have come to Ireland specially.'

The cliffs run along a stretch of coastline about eight kilometres long. It's hard to police. 'They come by bus, by taxi and by car.'

Not even COVID could stop the sad traffic. The Cliffs of Moher were shut during the pandemic, but managers still went into the visitors' centre. One Friday evening, one of them spotted a man near the cliff edge. 'She called the guards. It was all right.'

It is not always easy to identify suicidal people, Tom says. 'There was a girl. When we were walking together she kept one step back, she wouldn't come up beside me.' He demonstrates trying to walk beside a person while they persist in remaining out of step. It is awkward. 'Hindsight is a great thing.' The girl convinced him that she was all right, but later she jumped to her death.

Doolin Search and Rescue searches for missing people on land and sea. When the gardaí alert them to a possible suicide, the volunteers start the search on land, from the missing person's 'last known position'. The searchers are issued with strong torches. 'We'd search along the coastline. Then we search from the top of cliffs – you have more chance of seeing them from there. I've had good success with that.'

They sometimes find a suicidal person still on land. 'He might be sitting there, thinking about life.'

A body falling from the top of the cliffs takes about six seconds to reach the water, Tom says. It hits with such force that 'all the organs are pulled from their places'. Most people are dead before then, he says, because they hit outcrops of rock on their way down.

He remembers getting a phone call from the gardaí after a man had run away from a mental hospital in Dublin and was thought to be heading to the cliffs. He was successfully intercepted. But then, Tom says, he came back. 'We didn't see him the second time. Some people have seen people jumping over, but touch wood I've never seen that.'

The bodies float at first, but if they are not recovered quickly, they tend to sink, and then resurface after a few days. 'The tides and the currents here pull the bodies, and deliver the bodies, in every possible direction: north and south and west. To Connemara, to the Aran Islands. One time a body was carried to Dunquin, County Kerry, about a hundred and forty kilometres away by road.

'If it's rough, they're brought back in and smashed against the cliff. There was one man, you could see him being bashed against the rocks.'

Doolin Search and Rescue provides an inshore lifeboat service, which means it usually makes short journeys. It is very clear about its purpose when looking for someone who has been reported as missing. 'We're going out to recover somebody to give them back to their family. It's closure for them.'

Tom has met some of the bereaved families, and knows how desperate they are for identifying details. 'One time I said, "He had a little blue checked shirt on him with a Dunnes Stores label," and the woman said, "I bought that for him!"'

Once there was a woman he knew. A local woman. A nice woman. She often gave the lifeboat crew dinner when they came in from what Tom refers to as missions. 'I never thought it would be her.'

There are four or five crew members on the lifeboat, and after each mission they do a debrief. They talk about everything that happened from the time the call came in until the recovery of the body. 'One time a mother and child went off – that wasn't easy for the crew. People would have had children the same age.'

I wonder how this work might have changed him.

'I suppose it gives me more of an insight into people. More of a connection with the people who are left behind, meeting them afterwards. I know one woman who came up and she just wanted to walk in the last place her son had walked. People want to know the exact place where it happened. It's a place of great beauty and it's a place of great sadness.'

Tom doesn't think much about his own death. 'When my number comes up, that's it. A heart attack maybe.' In all his years on the sea, he has never felt in any imminent danger.

'Not really. Even though I've been in heavy situations. Even when we went to see that film, *The Perfect Storm*, and two days later we were called out for someone who had gone missing in Lahinch and all you could see was walls of green water. You never beat nature. You've got to know when to go and when to stop.'

He spends his time watching the sea. 'I've always been on the sea. And walking the shore, watching the sea – where the swells are. I often heard the old people in town say, "Never turn your back on the sea."'

The Talk

Jobstown is a working-class suburb in south-west Dublin, tucked between Tallaght and the Dublin Mountains. In the late afternoon of 2 March 2018, when Ireland was in the grip of a major snowstorm, a gang of men arrived at the local Lidl in a mechanical digger and broke in. After they spent some hours looting the store, the digger smashed the walls and roof: this gave the raiders access to the safe, though they were unable to open it. In a time of national emergency, this event left the country rather impressed – and the people of Jobstown furious. They were aware that their area was known for deprivation and crime, and they were at pains to say that none of the raiders was local. 'Two of them were from the north side. One of them was from Shankill,' one man told me. 'I don't know what he was doing up here.'

The following Tuesday, a group of people met in the

Jobstown House pub to train in suicide prevention. In the preceding five months, there had been seventeen suicides in the area.

'It felt like one a week,' says John Kilbride, the young proprietor of the pub. When his grandfather, Thomas Kilbride, moved out to Jobstown from the inner city, the pub was effectively an agricultural supplier for the local farmers. 'There was one shelf of drink,' says John. Now Jobstown House is a big modern pub, and we are here amongst the few morning drinkers. In three generations of the Kilbride proprietorship, the place has become a social centre for a modern urban community that has never been a priority for planners, for landscapers or for the people who provide the bus services.

The men who had initiated the suicide prevention training were Jeff O'Toole, who is a youth worker, and Frank Stacey, who is the trainer at the local Westside Boxing Club. Jeff is very small and Frank is very big. They are both in their early forties and, crucially, both grew up in Jobstown, arriving in the area as babies in 1981, when their families moved from public housing elsewhere in the city. Frank still lives here, with his wife and three children. Jeff now lives in neighbouring Fettercairn, though his parents, brother and two of his sisters still live in Jobstown.

It was his friendship with Frank that inspired Jeff to do something about the suicide rate in Jobstown. One of the recent suicides had been that of a young teenager, a member of Frank's boxing club, who had hanged himself on the local golf course.

'It was hurting him, I could see it,' Jeff says.

'He boxed for me,' says Frank of the boy. 'And I was speaking to him and speaking to him, and I didn't know.'

The two men were out for a drink in Jobstown House, and Frank said to Jeff, 'If only I had known, I could have done something.

'And Jeff said to me, "Did you not see any of the flare signs?"'

When Frank was young, there were two boxing clubs in the area. 'Richie Kavanagh had the first gym – St Thomas's Boxing Club. And Paddy Hyland had the Golden Cobra. Paddy unfortunately committed suicide. Very flamboyant, Pat. He was great for the area, he helped a lot of kids. What makes anybody do what they do? He split up from his wife after years. He had three boys who boxed in the professional game. His life was pretty good. He killed himself in 2015. We were all asking why.'

The death of Paddy Hyland was not Frank's first experience of suicide. In 2002, his sister, Catherine, killed herself.

Catherine had become addicted to heroin. 'She was on drugs for a few years. Then she was on the local drug programme . . . You count how many drug centres there are in Tallaght. There's one for every area in Tallaght. There's one for Brookfield. There's one for Glenshane. There's one for Jobstown. There's one for Fettercairn. There's one for Killinarden. They're everywhere. Now you ask yourself: how many youth clubs are there? How many playgrounds?

'Do the drug centres work? In my opinion, no. I've a

friend coming off drugs the last fifteen years. He's still on Physeptone [i.e. methadone] – how can that be?'

Catherine attended one of the drug centres for about a year and a half, and was then given a place on a residential drug rehabilitation programme. 'She came into my ma's house all excited and said, "I'm after getting the course! I'm after getting the residential!"'

At the time, Frank was newly married to his wife, Christine, and their son, Sean, was a baby. They had just moved into their new house in the Glenshane estate in Jobstown. Catherine's residential course would not begin for six weeks. She needed a home address in the area in order to qualify for it, and because Frank's mother had four other children to consider, she went to live with Frank and Christine – and to undergo heroin withdrawal with them.

'Christine and Catherine got on very well. Christine was great with Catherine – helping her when she got sick. We had to lock the doors, we had to lock the windows. Catherine was bouncing off the walls, screaming, crying. To listen to someone you love and care for go through that . . . Though my father did warn me. He said, "Do you know what you're in for, son?" But he did give me all the advice. He told me how to help her – the hot cloths. Everything what to do. So he was in the wings without Catherine knowing, rooting for her in a major, major way.

'And it was nice for my ma to come to the house and to see her sitting round in the living room with Christine, talking – a proper conversation, instead of "Did she take this? And did this happen?" It was nice. It reminded her of us of years ago. It was normal. But the major fact was that my father and Catherine hadn't spoken for years. And yeah, they sat in the kitchen together for nearly three hours. I don't know what was said. But it was beautiful. It was nice just to see that connection.'

Frank remembers a conversation he had with Catherine when they were watching TV. 'She said to me: "You know, this life is not for me. This, like, being in a car, freezing. Scrounging for drugs. Robbing for drugs. You know, I'm way better than this. It's just the shame I've brought on all of us."

'And she said it to me lying on that couch: "If I don't do it now, Frank, this world isn't for me."'

Having successfully withdrawn from heroin, Catherine left Frank and Christine's house and entered the residential drug rehabilitation programme. Her stay was not a success.

'It put her back in that environment, around that mentality. Within a month or two she knocked on our door and she said, "I should be the first to tell you, I'm back using."'

Eighteen months later, she was living in homeless accommodation on the North Circular Road. She maintained a good relationship with both her parents, who provided her with household items and groceries. Her father drove her places. They helped her as much as they could.

Frank learned of Catherine's death from his father. He weeps as he remembers the suffering Catherine's death brought.

'To be somebody on the inside, to experience suicide at first hand, is something that I wouldn't wish upon my worst enemy. That hurt. That pain. There's so many emotions that go with it. You're angry at them. The world. You're looking at your parents devastated.

'I think death is a test of what type of person you are. It's easy for me to get drunk, to do stupid things, feel sorry for myself – that's easy. The hard thing to do is to face it. And it is a process. I think the ultimate test, for any person, is to lose a child. I've seen my parents and I admire the way they deal with it. I think it gave them an insight into the depths of death. I've watched them. Because it beat my ma. It beat my ma. The death of my sister beat my mother. Because she got sick. She could never get out of that slump, let's say. Every now and then she would be great again. It's the guilt.'

Frank thinks his work at the boxing club saved him from falling into a depression after Catherine's death.

'We've a hall full of kids and young lads training . . . I see people who are looking forward, looking to their future. At sixteen or seventeen, you think you're unstoppable. That's great to see. It's brilliant. Last night I was out in Ballybrack. We brought out twenty of our kids to do a bit of sparring. Like nine, ten, eleven, twelve years of age. Just to watch them. No fear.'

Jeff O'Toole knew about the concept of the 'flare signs' of suicide because, as a social worker, he had been trained in Safetalk, a suicide prevention programme. After getting the training, he realized 'that our guards didn't have the training, our nurses didn't have the training, our doctors didn't have the training. So if someone came into this pub showing signs of distress, our initial reaction is to ring the guards – but the guards aren't trained to accommodate it.'

Frank and Jeff drew up a list of people within the

community whom they knew had direct contact with young people: teachers, coaches, people running clubs in karate and chess and drama and the choir.

'We wanted to protect the young people first,' says Jeff. 'We got, I think it was, twenty-seven to attend the training. I didn't ring them, I actually called to see them. I don't like phones. I don't like texting, all that message stuff. I'd rather talk to people face to face. Because it's easy to say "Yeah, I want to do something" over the phone. But when you're asking someone and you have an opportunity to explain why we're doing it, they can't get away. They have to listen.'

So it was that just after that JCB destroyed the local Lidl, the first suicide prevention training took place in Jobstown House.

When I attended a training session, people were told to look for signs of distress – a change in behaviour or even in grooming. 'After the training, I was spotting things,' says John Kilbride. 'People don't come out and say it. They might say "Work is really bad." Or "I've got a big bill coming up." Before the training I would have said "That's terrible" and moved on. Now I know what to say.' If there are worrying signs, the next step is to ask the person a series of questions, leading up to asking if they are contemplating suicide. John, who has now done this a number of times, still finds it very scary. He slaps his chest as he mimics his pounding heart and says, 'Oh my God, I can't believe I'm going to ask if they're suicidal.'

This is precisely what volunteers all over Jobstown now do, all the time.

Once it is established that a person is indeed having suicidal thoughts, they are referred to a counsellor. John reckons he has performed between ten and fifteen suicide interventions in his pub. 'We had one man here, the pub was his only outlet, and he couldn't believe that the staff had noticed he was in trouble. And he came in afterwards and gave them all hugs.'

Frank Stacey felt the effect of the training immediately, in his work at Westside Boxing Club.

'The training made me more aware . . . With me, when I get to know someone very, very well, I listen to their tone. Their demeanour. Like when they're on the bag: how hard they're hitting it. You've a lad on the bag and normally, nine times out of ten, he's poncing about and he's tipping it. But then you see him on another night and he's really nailing that bag, and he's saying nothing. You can see by the way he does his push-ups, by the way he's doing his sit-ups. So then another time you see a kid that's excellent on the bags and now he's not pushed.

'So it's easy for me then to walk over: "Everything okay with you?"

'And to say that to a kid, nine times out of ten he'll say, "Yeah, yeah, yeah."

'So you leave them, bring over a bottle of water and have a chat with them: "What did you do today?" Then he'll tell you, one to one.

'I do say to every kid in the club: "When youse are in this gym and in this boxing ring I have to treat youse the same way I treat my son, Sean. I have to do what's best by youse.

So if you think you need to talk, speak to me. If you need anything in the world, if you're having trouble in school, you can talk." We're very open about that these days. You have to be. You get them at a young age now and let them know they can talk. Whereas before, when I was growing up, you kept it all in.'

After that first Safetalk training session in Jobstown House in March 2018, Jeff O'Toole was left with a bit of a problem. 'I thought, what's the point in training people in the community if no one knows who has the training?' So they shot videos in which those who had been trained identified themselves. 'We showed the people face-on. "This is who I am. I'm Jeff O'Toole and it's safe to talk to me." "I'm Frank Stacey from Westside Boxing Club and it's safe to talk to me." "I'm John Kilbride from Jobstown House and it's safe to talk to me." And so on.' They put the videos out on social media. 'People in the community really embraced it, and they started having the conversations with people they'd seen on the video. Then they contacted me and said: "We want to do that training."'

I spoke to Jeff and Frank and John a year after the initial training in Jobstown House. During the intervening year, according to Jeff, there had not been a single suicide in Jobstown.

How did he feel about this success?

'I felt mixed. I felt proud, obviously. I felt proud. And I felt disappointed that it took two members of the community, just two normal lads, two Joes, to come up with this. I felt a bit let down – not personally, but as a community.'

Of the seventy-five or eighty people who had done the training to that point, Jeff reckoned that two thirds of them had made interventions.

Some Travellers in Donegal, having seen Jobstown's Safe-talk video on Facebook, got Safetalk training for their community. The suicide rate among Travellers is some six times higher than in the general population, and Jeff had worked with Travellers as a youth worker for seven years in Tallaght. That was his first experience of seeing suicide reaching epidemic levels.

Through his discussions with the young Travellers, and with their parents, he learned that they would often have concerns about someone on the halting site – 'about his mental health, that he was showing suicidal tendencies. But no one was intervening. They were trying in their own way, but it wasn't necessarily the right way. And these people went on to complete suicide. I thought, "These people knew this was going to happen and they're trying their best to stop it. Why is no one helping them?"'

After the success of the Jobstown Safetalk programme, the Health Services Executive asked Jeff if he and Frank could do something similar in other targeted areas. 'I think eventually – and probably better late than never, I suppose – they've realized that people sitting round a table isn't going to fix this. It has to start here. It has to start in the community. If we're the ones affected by it, we're the ones that can fix it.'

Of course, the programme was never going to eliminate suicide in the area completely. Jeff would later tell me, shortly before this book went to press, that there had been a total of seven suicides in Jobstown in the three years following the launch of the Safetalk programme.

But the carnage of 2017–18 had been arrested. Jeff believes that the Jobstown Safetalk programme has been effective because, although suicidal people are eventually referred to professionals by the practitioners on the ground, it is not mediated by experts. Suicidal people, he says, are 'not asking professionals for help, they're asking their next-door neighbour for help, because their next-door neighbour has had that little bit of training. They're asking their football manager. They're having a conversation with the butcher.' (Tony, who works at the local butcher's shop, completed the training.) 'They're having a conversation with the barman, they're having the conversation with the choir teacher who might have noticed something's wrong.'

To the outside observer, the most striking feature of the Jobstown community's initiative – apart from its success – is that it grew and thrived without any type of funding. Indeed, it is specifically anti-funding.

Frank Stacey remembers that on the very first night of Safetalk training, back in March 2018, one young woman arrived 'with a basket from the chemist'. It was a gift hamper of products that the young woman expected would be raffled to raise money for the project. Ireland has a strong tradition of voluntary community projects, often supported by various forms of fundraising. But instead of holding a raffle, the organizers of the Safetalk training sent the basket back to the chemist who had donated it, saying, according to Frank,

'Thanks a million, we really appreciate it, but you know what would mean more to us? If youse came and done the course in the next batch. Because we're going to keep going.'

Frank says, 'We agreed from the start: we're going to do this with no money. Because you hear of all these organizations, and they're set up, I think, with great intent. I think they just get misled then.' Part of it, he says, is the simple fact that 'We don't need funding.' It's a straightforward programme. They have people who are willing to volunteer their time. They don't need offices or supplies.

Jeff says, 'I decided from the start I didn't want any political input, I didn't want any organizational input, I didn't want charitable input.' He feels it was the right call in hindsight. 'If we had had a politician there, or if we had had governmental funding there, it wouldn't have been ours – it wouldn't have been Jobstown's. And now, because of the success of it, every politician in Jobstown has contacted me. So I put it back on them and I said, "If you're really interested in Safetalk, I'll arrange a Safetalk programme for every politician in Jobstown to attend as a participant, and let's see if you're serious about it."'

8

Liam O'Flynn

16 March 2018

In the Eurospar shop in the small village of Kill in County Kildare, there is a long queue for coffee, and a succession of slightly dazed-looking men coming out of the toilets: Irish traditional musicians are not generally early risers. The sign for the Dew Drop Inn gastropub swings in the breeze. But Millie's Barbershop is closed because it is Cheltenham week, and this is the heart of horse-racing country.

A woman has been standing in the cold outside the church for at least forty minutes, guarding a book of condolence. 'For Jane,' she says. Jane is Liam O'Flynn's widow. She was a renowned eventer, and is now a trainer. The couple met on the gallops at the Curragh; horses were for Liam O'Flynn an enduring love.

The church is L-shaped, and its interior, unusually for an Irish church, is painted in a tasteful neutral colour that could be Bone by Farrow & Ball. To the left of the altar there are three or four pipers sitting on a row of chairs. Also the fiddler Sean Keane, of the Chieftains. And Dónal Lunny, one of the founder members of the Irish trad band Planxty, of which Liam Óg (as he was known to his family) was also a founder. The altar is so crowded with musicians that is hard to see everyone. The pipers, as ever, look smart. Liam

O'Flynn was a master piper, the most famous piper of his generation. He was also a petrolhead with a love of motorbikes and cars. And a boxing fan. And a single-digit-handicap golfer.

The wicker coffin arrives to the sound of a lone piper, a sound that could tear your heart from your body. It is the air 'Táimse im'chodladh is ná dúistear mé', played by Gay McKeon, who is the chief executive of Na Píobairí Uilleann, the organization formed in 1968 to make sure the uilleann pipes did not die out.

The uilleann pipes, powered by bellows rather than breath, are the whale of Irish traditional music. They lurk under everything and then break the surface with a great surge of energy that rivets you with either sorrow or the urge to dance. Here they evoke sadness and a sense of desolation.

The man who was in charge of the parking – with a system uniquely his own, but which was justified in the end – comes in the side door to listen. There are guitars in the mix now, and with the drumming and the piping someone lets out a yelp of encouragement.

Iarla Ó Lionáird, a sean-nós singer, sings 'Seán Ó Duibhir a'Ghleanna'.

There is a reading from the Second Letter of Paul to Timothy.

Christy Moore, who was in Planxty, is sitting with the other musicians on the left of the altar, wearing a black T-shirt with long sleeves. He is probably Ireland's most beloved singer – once described by John S. Doyle as 'integrity in a vest'.

There is a reading from the Gospel of St Matthew.

Then Father Willie O'Byrne gives the sermon. He talks about how Liam O'Flynn was from this very village. His father, also Liam, who was a fiddler, had been the principal of the local national school here, and his mother, Maisie, had been in charge of the choir. (Maisie was from Clare, piping country, and was a cousin of a famous fiddler, Junior Cregan.)

Now the priest is saying that Liam later attended a boarding school in Carlow that he himself also attended. 'Let me tell you, he never changed,' says Father O'Byrne. 'Illness struck him eight years ago. He was my own age so I regard him as a young man still.' Liam O'Flynn died at seventy-two.

Father O'Byrne invites us to stand up for the Our Father, and it is interesting how many of the musicians next to the altar do not stand. Someone plays 'Seán Óg' by Seán Ó Riada on the flute.

Liam O'Flynn was a precise, disciplined man who, after Planxty's fiery break-ups – there was more than one – went on to work with the experimental composer John Cage, as well as Mark Knopfler and Kate Bush and Emmylou Harris, and also with Seamus Heaney for a series of live performances and an album called *The Poet and the Piper*. In 1999, he played from his album *The Piper's Call* at the BBC Proms in the Royal Albert Hall in London. Not for him the alcoholism and chaos that engulfed other masters of Irish traditional music. Like, for example, the piper Seamus Ennis, to whom Liam O'Flynn was close as a young man. Seamus Ennis was his mentor and he left him his pipes when he died.

Christy Moore starts to sing 'The Cliffs of Dooneen'. In the middle he says quietly, 'We'll sing it now', and the whole congregation joins in with this gentle song. The line 'Fare thee well for a while' comes in from the body of the church in predominantly female voices. It is sweet.

Now one of the musicians, Paddy Glackin, a fiddler and Liam O'Flynn's great friend, gives the oration in a tweed jacket and blue shirt and a tie. The thing about Liam, he says, was that like other great musicians, he had *draíocht* – magic. 'He understood simplicity in a way few people do. He understood space. He understood silence.'

I am thinking of Liam O'Flynn sitting amongst the long hair, the beards and the sweat of the other Planxty musicians in a nicely ironed shirt. He had a Zen-like concentration about him.

In an interview with John Kelly in 1998, Liam said this about performing: 'When I'm playing, I'm certainly lost within it. The only way to describe it is that it's like looking inwards. And if I try to facially or physically make contact with people, I lose it. It interferes with the physical business of playing. I think when a performer engages with the audience and vice versa it's like a spell is cast and a terrific passage of feelings moves from the musician to the audience and back again. What you're doing is that you're after something in the tune and, at the end of the day, you're just the servant of the music. Seamus Ennis gave me much more than just a bag of notes.'

The singers are singing off sheets now.

The pipes are droning together in sadness.

In the side aisle an entire string quartet is lining up behind the drummer, waiting for their turn. They are here to play extracts from *The Brendan Voyage*, on which Liam O'Flynn collaborated with the composer Sean Davey.

At the end, they play 'The Gold Ring', one of Liam's signature tunes. It is unusual to be at a funeral where there is more music than anything else. This was not just the funeral of a musician, it was a musicians' funeral, and it ran on their respect for the dead man.

Afterwards, a small group drives out of the village, back towards Dublin, to the Newlands crematorium. Once we are there, Father O'Byrne says, 'We're just waiting for the musicians.' Paul Brady slips in with his guitar. Dónal Lunny is on bouzouki this time. Gay McKeon straps on the pipes again: getting the uilleann pipes on you is a bit like putting on a bra; you have to slip your arms through the straps. Paddy Glackin helps to carry the coffin. Once it has been put on the plinth, he takes out his fiddle. There are about five fiddles now.

It is difficult to say what Planxty meant to people in the seventies: the attack of the music, the excellence of the musicianship, the roar of sophistication they brought to Irish traditional music and to their audience, who were dressed in Afghan coats and fur coats and uncomfortable clogs. We listened to their albums to the purr of the gas fires in our damp flats and bedsits. Planxty helped an entire generation to rethink its past; to connect with something that had nothing to do with the shabbiness of Ireland back then.

Here in the crematorium, the musicians are really in

charge now. Out in the car park they have, some of them, left expensive cars, but inside it is as if the past forty years have never happened. The sisters Maighread and Tríona Ní Dhomhnaill sing 'Bánchnoic Éireann', and Tríona plays a little electronic keyboard. There are no microphones. When they have finished, you have never heard a silence like it. Tríona Ní Domhnaill played the clavinet in the Bothy Band with, at various times, Dónal Lunny and Paddy Glackin and Liam O'Flynn. The family tree of Irish traditional music in the seventies and eighties was small but very convoluted.

Father O'Byrne is now saying that we will have a decade of the Rosary. The musicians mostly sit it out. When it is over, Paddy Glackin takes up his bow. The coffin starts to move, to be taken away. The panelled doors close behind it. It is gone. And the music comes as a type of comfort. There are three or four pipers, working hard. And the fiddles. And Seamus Begley on accordion. And Angela Crehan on the tin whistle. One piper glances over his shoulder to look at something behind him, like a man reversing a car. Paddy Glackin moves into another tune. They stop and Dónal Lunny says, 'We'll do one more', and the fiddles are brought out again for a selection of reels. You couldn't send people out with that much sadness.

Liam O'Flynn

1945–2018

9

Remembering

Peter Tyrrell

Peter Tyrrell, an Irishman from County Galway, died by setting fire to himself on Hampstead Heath on 26 April 1967.

Over the previous four years, starting with the death of
Thich Quang Duc in Saigon in June 1963, there had been a
number of deaths by self-immolation in Vietnam, and other
places, in protest against the American war there. The
American photographer Malcolm Browne had recorded
Thich Quang Duc's death as the monk sat motionless in the
flames, having been doused with petrol by another monk,
and having lit the fire himself with a single match as soon as
he had finished chanting to Amida Buddha. He was dead
within ten minutes, without a cry, his body falling backwards. His fellow monks had brought a coffin with them,
and placed his body in it. But the body had become rigid
during the conflagration and they could not get one of the
arms down into the coffin, so that it protruded as the corpse
was driven away to its funeral – a second burning.

Meanwhile, Malcolm Browne had given his roll of film to
someone who was flying to America, where the photographs
caused consternation. Thich Quang Duc had been protesting
against the anti-Buddhist laws enacted by the American-backed

Diem regime in Vietnam. In a way that Peter Tyrrell might have appreciated, his self-immolation was a protest against the Catholic Church. The Roman Catholic president of Vietnam at that time, Ngo Dinh Diem, whose brother was an archbishop, had forbidden the flying of Buddhist flags on the Buddha's birthday the previous month, but the Vatican flag was flown freely.

Before his own death, Peter Tyrrell had been conducting a protest campaign for more than ten years, against the mistreatment of children in Ireland's industrial schools. Crucially, he had no fear of death. In his posthumously published book, *Founded on Fear*, he wrote of his experiences at the industrial school run by the Christian Brothers in Letterfrack, County Galway: 'I made up my mind that life was not worth living. I wanted to die.' When he saw the dead body of a fellow inmate, who had died in an accident while transporting coal to the industrial school, he felt the boy 'looked better dead than alive, he looked happy and perfectly relaxed, his face was no longer drawn in pain, as I had so often seen before, the lines had gone from under his eyes, he seemed as though about to smile. From then onwards I thought of death as a reward for having lived, something to be desired, a prize for having accomplished an ambition.'

Peter Tyrrell was fifty-one when he died. It took the London police a year to identify his body. As part of their investigation, they tried to identify the name on a charred postcard found in the pocket of a dead man. They deciphered the name Owen Sheehy-Skeffington, an academic, Labour Party activist and sometime senator who had campaigned against corporal punishment in Irish schools. It was the final note in a correspondence between the two men. Sheehy-Skeffington had encouraged Tyrrell to write down his memories of his childhood. Unlike most people who receive such encouragement, Tyrrell not only undertook the project, but completed it. He wrote after long days at his job as a tailor, and at weekends. Anyone who has seen the manuscript will know that it is a remarkably fluid work and, in its frankness, remarkably modern.

The manuscript would not be published until 2006, after being found among Sheehy-Skeffington's papers. The story it has to tell, which begins in the family home outside the village of Ahascragh in east Galway, is as vivid as, and a great deal more horrifying than, anything in Dickens. Tyrrell described his father as someone who was always helpful and active on behalf of his neighbours, but 'at home he was a lazy and irresponsible husband and father'.

The Tyrrells were effectively destitute. 'We have four acres of good land which has not been tilled for years and yet Dad prays every day and asks Almighty God to provide for us. There is no turf for the fire, although we have more than twelve acres of first-class bog.'

The Tyrrell children lived from hand to mouth, pulling potatoes and turnips from the ground 'to survive one more day', as well as relying on the indulgence of their neighbours and occasional remittances sent by relatives in America. Their mother supported the family by begging and borrowing from the neighbours. She had come from a fine two-storey whitewashed house in County Roscommon, which, she told

Peter, had forty acres of land. When she was twenty-two, she had been matched at the October Ballinasloe Fair to his father. In her new marital home they had to 'travel over a mile for water'. By the time she was thirty-eight, she was the mother of ten children.

Peter liked school. 'The teacher Mrs Kennedy gave us lunch each day which she brought from her own home . . . She also gave us a sweet every day.' But the time came when the Tyrrell boys could no longer go to school, because they had no clothes to wear. It was their non-attendance, perhaps combined with the effects of Mrs Tyrrell's last confinement and painful rheumatism, that led to six of her children, including Peter, being sent away to institutions.

On the day of their departure, 'I remember well my Mother washing my face with a dishrag, and telling me not to be lonely. She was saying between sobs that we were going to nice Christian people.' The boys were picked up by police officers, who could not get their car up the narrow boreen to the house. As the party of gardaí and small boys walked to the main road, Peter suddenly heard cries: 'Mother was running to try and catch up with us when she stumbled and fell to the ground. Mother had been bad on her legs since the baby was born.'

He and three of his brothers were sent to St Joseph's Industrial School at Letterfrack on the west coast of Galway. His two younger brothers were sent to an industrial school 'for junior boys' in Kilkenny. Peter Tyrrell was eight years old when he left home. The year was 1924. He would not see his mother again for seven years.

At Letterfrack, the children were beaten all the time. Although they showered often – they were beaten in the showers, too – their clothes were never washed and were infested with lice. Peter had his arm broken while trying to ward off a beating, and he was instructed to tell the doctor that he had fallen down the stairs. There were seventy-two beds in each dormitory, and the boys were beaten if they were awake in the morning ahead of schedule: 'It's a crime to be awake before we are called.'

There were some decent and kindly brothers, like Brother Byrne, who told the children, 'There is no one who is qualified to replace your own mother' and was frank about their prospects of abject failure on reaching adulthood: 'You will always be identified by your sheepish look.'

By his sixth year at Letterfrack, Peter had stopped writing home. 'I have not received a letter because I have not answered the last two letters from home. Now I know why many of the other lads stopped writing. I now feel bitter towards my parents. I want to write home and tell them everything, but always change my mind at the last moment. I now feel glad I never wrote. I think it's much better that my parents forget about me. I shall soon be fifteen.'

By this point he has sewn a double layer of stout material into his trousers to protect his bottom – 'We are usually beaten four times a day' – and he has plans to reinforce his jacket in a similar way, to protect his shoulders from the cane. He is promising other boys that he can do the same for them. But he is also sweating and fearful and unable to concentrate on his lessons. He comes second last in an exam and has to wear the dunce's cap. His hands are sometimes so damaged by beatings that he cannot work at his tailoring. His younger brother, Laurence, has now arrived at Letterfrack – presumably having graduated from the Kilkenny institution – but Peter does not recognize him. Laurence's chilblains become septic and have to be lanced.

Eventually Peter returned home, because his father had found him a job at the local tailor's.

It was not a happy homecoming. He did not recognize his father, who had come to meet him. His mother, pathetically, said to him: 'I thought there was something wrong. You have only written twice in the last two years. How could you forget me?'

Tyrrell's parents can hardly be blamed for not being able to imagine what their children had endured at Letterfrack. But their blithe expectation that normal relations could be resumed was bitter indeed.

On his return from Letterfrack, Peter found that he was afraid of his neighbours: 'I hardly spoke to anyone, except my mother.'

A local girl, Peggy, whom he is interested in, is told that he has been in Letterfrack. After this, Peter writes, 'She wouldn't look at me anymore.'

He goes home over the fields in order to avoid the eyes of his neighbours. But his own eyes are as sharp as ever, now turned on the regime of his home village. 'I have now noticed how dirty people are . . . The suffering of animals is appalling.'

He sees how a local man called Cliss, 'a simpleton', is

thrown off his cart by the young men of the village each day and made to spill the milk that is carried on it, and how people come out to watch the spectacle.

Ballinasloe, the nearest town, now has its own mental hospital, and a member of its staff is a customer of the tailor for whom Peter works. 'He says that they had several patients from a Christian Brothers school who were troublesome and difficult to handle.' The staff are not allowed to hit an inmate, the man says, but he then laughs and adds, 'there are other patients who do the job for us'.

Peter's younger brother Jack comes home 'extremely nervous' and illiterate. Jack is aggressive and sometimes disappears for days, drinking.

Of his wages of ten shillings a week, Peter gives eight to his mother and saves the rest to join his brother Paddy in London. There, he joins the army and likes it. During the war he is wounded and taken prisoner by the Germans. He is in a prisoner of war camp at Fallingbostel, near Hanover. The faces of the prisoners remind him of the boys in Letterfrack, but unlike in Letterfrack, he and his fellow inmates are not mistreated.

On returning to civilian life, Peter Tyrrell received a postcard from home to tell him that his mother was dead and that, his father having died a few years earlier, the farm had been sold.

'As I had little or nothing to do with my family for many years I felt no great sorrow. On the contrary I was relieved. My mother had been ill for as long as I can remember . . . During the few years I spent at home after leaving school

[Letterfrack] I used to wonder how long my mother would have to go on living. She was suffering terribly and would cry most of the night. It was then I began to look upon death as a companion and true friend.'

After the war, Peter became part of the huge Irish community in Britain. He was beaten up several times by Irishmen for arguing against the dominance of the Church and Ireland's Anglophobia, and above all for criticizing the Christian Brothers. 'Former pupils don't want to be reminded of the past,' he wrote.

But Peter refused to forget. In 1953, he wrote twice to the superior at Letterfrack detailing abuses by three brothers – including an account of how he used to be brought into the pantry by Brother Vale, forced to strip and flogged. The superior never replied. He wrote to the superior general of the Christian Brothers. He visited their headquarters in Dublin to confront them with his account of abuses at Letterfrack, but was dismissed by them, in a subsequent letter to their solicitors, as 'being on a blackmail ticket'. He wrote to the Taoiseach, Seán Lemass, and to the President, Éamon de Valera. He wrote to the Archbishop of Westminster and to the *News of the World*.

He sent Owen Sheehy-Skeffington his book piece by piece, from 1958 to 1965, each instalment sewn together with his tailor's hand. He told Sheehy-Skeffington that he was troubled by the things he could not remember, and by things 'too terrible to put in writing which I can remember'.

There is no mention in *Founded on Fear* of sexual abuse:

this was, perhaps, one of the things too terrible for Peter Tyrrell to remember in print. Through the Irish Centre in London, he was put in touch with Tuairim, a group of Irish intellectuals who were producing reports of various aspects of Irish society. He told the Tuairim group of the experiences outlined in his book and also, according to the historian Daire Keogh, that he had been raped at Letterfrack. And that he had been rebuked by a priest for lying when he brought this outrage up during confession. Peter Tyrrell was on the committee that was in charge of producing Tuairim's subsequent report on 'residential care of the deprived', published in 1966, but none of his testimony was included in it.

The writer Dermot Bolger has said that it was this final rejection, by the Irish intelligentsia, that was the last straw for Tyrrell. He killed himself the following year, in his own blaze on Hampstead Heath, unseen.

The allegations made by Peter Tyrrell against the Christian Brothers have never been refuted. His accusations of cruelty and sexual abuse at Letterfrack were included in the Ryan Report, published in 2009, which confirmed them. There is no other memorial to him, either in Ireland or in London. There have been informal gatherings at the site of his suicide on Hampstead Heath on the anniversary of his death, but no regular commemorations. I was told by the authorities in London that even the record of the inquest into his death had been destroyed in a general reorganization of records. He left no other writings. But his death and his book were political acts: his body was all he had to burn.

The Graves of Bellaghy

As you enter the village of Bellaghy, County Derry, a peculiar structure catches the eye: a piece of contemporary
architecture, vaguely evocative of a gabled farmhouse or
agricultural shed, but on a disorientingly large scale. This is
the museum known as the Seamus Heaney HomePlace. Here
you can look at Heaney's duffel coat in a glass vitrine, with
its checked lining, and three of its four toggles gone. There
are two more duffel coats – one child-sized – upstairs in the
Creative Zone, where you can try them on.

There is so much poetry here that everything starts to
look like poetry. In the ladies' toilet, a sign on one of the
hand dryers saying 'Out of Order' has me thinking about it
for quite a while. Upstairs in the café, you can get coffee and
very large brownies, and they let you use their phones –
mobile coverage north of the border can be patchy for
southerners.

And southerners love Seamus Heaney. When he died in
August 2013, there was a minute's silence held at that year's
All-Ireland football semi-final in Croke Park. Besides being
a poet who had won the Nobel Prize, he seemed like a good
man, who liked us. We like people who like us.

Bellaghy is in eastern County Derry, just north of Lough
Neagh – geographically closer to Belfast than to Derry city.
The village – one street and several churches and a butcher
that calls itself a flesher's – is not technically Seamus Heaney's
homeplace. He was born on a farm in a place called

Mossbawn, a couple of miles away. His father then inherited another farm from an uncle and the Heaney family moved to the other side of Bellaghy, to a farm called the Wood.

Bellaghy has the quietness of many small Northern Ireland towns. You can see that Seamus Heaney is the best thing that has ever happened to this place, a connection that is being used to bring some fresh life and economic activity to the area. What would Heaney, sophisticated and strategic, the man who once said that the act of writing was an escape from self-obsession, have thought of it all? My friend Marian, who has travelled with me, says, 'He would have been tactful.' She got to sleep in the Seamus Heaney room of our B&B last night, under a portrait of him. 'The Child That's Due' was framed outside her bathroom. I was in the Michael Longley and slept between 'Homecoming' and 'Gorse Fires'. And our friend Charlie was in the Patrick Kavanagh: 'Memory of My Father', and 'A Christmas Childhood' as you came in the door. Seamus Heaney had visited that B&B, knew its owners, and must have realized long before his death that he was on his way to becoming a tourist attraction.

Marian and I went into a pub in Bellaghy, two women together (Charlie was elsewhere), so naturally we got talking to three local men, and they helped us decide where to eat: it was between the Chinese and the chipper. It's not easy finding places to eat in an Irish village early on a Sunday evening. We started to talk about the Seamus Heaney Home-Place, and the nice local men, these lovely local men with their tans and their laughter, said that Seamus Heaney was not the only great man to come from Bellaghy. Oh really, we said politely. No indeed, they said. There was also Francis Hughes.

'Francis Hughes as in IRA Francis Hughes?' I said. That's right, they said. He's buried in the local graveyard.

Francis Hughes died in 1981, at the age of twenty-five. He lies now under a huge horizontal slab of polished black stone. He was implicated in many murders. (The police said that he was responsible for thirty; republican sources said it was more than a dozen.) He was held to be an expert at the construction of booby trap bombs, using domestic clothes pegs as the central trigger – clothes pegs were once manufactured in Bellaghy, and the best wood from which to make them, a local history pamphlet says, is lime. He seemed nerveless to the point of recklessness. One IRA commander said of him, 'He was the sort of man who would shoot up a few policemen on his way to a meeting to plan our next attack on the police.' He planted bombs around Bellaghy in shops and a garage, shouting 'Up the Provies' as he ran away.

The most terrible killing in which Francis Hughes was implicated was that of a grandmother, Hester McMullan, who was murdered when the IRA raked her home at Toomebridge with gunfire, firing at least twenty-eight shots. She was a Protestant, and one of her children was an RUC reservist. One of the four guns used in the attack was discovered with Francis Hughes when he was captured.

In 1978, he was apprehended after a shootout with two British soldiers, who were possibly from the SAS, and one of whom, Lance Corporal David Jones, was killed in the exchange. Hughes himself was badly wounded in the hip, and he was ten months in hospital before he was well enough to be tried. He was sentenced to eighty-three years in prison.

In Long Kesh, he got a reputation as a fine singer. He was the second IRA prisoner to join the 1981 hunger strike, after Bobby Sands, and he died after fifty-nine days without food.

Upon his death there was heavy rioting, and a series of rows over the route of the funeral to Bellaghy. At one point a crowd surrounded the cortège and shouted, 'We'll take the Fenian bastard and burn him in a ditch.' The police refused to allow it to pass through Bellaghy, the town Hughes had so enthusiastically bombed years before.

Also buried in the local graveyard is Francis Hughes' cousin, Thomas McElwee. The two of them grew up within yards of each other in the townland of Tamlaghtduff, out on the Scribe Road. Thomas McElwee's mother gave birth to sixteen children, of whom twelve survived. Like Hughes, McElwee was good with his hands. The Bobby Sands Trust states that he was part of 'successful bomb blitzes' in Magherafelt, Bellaghy, Castledawson and Maghera. His family, like most rural families at that time, was religious. On 8 October 1976, a 'station Mass' was being held in the McElwee home. The next day the family received a phone call to say that both Thomas and his brother Benedict were in the Waverley hospital in Ballymena. Bombs that they had been bringing to Ballymena had exploded prematurely. Thomas had lost an eye. Another IRA man lost his leg above the knee. Benedict, a year younger than Thomas at eighteen years of age, had sustained a perforated eardrum. A coat was found in the bombers' car, and in it was a list of the shops that were proposed bombing targets.

An hour later, there was an explosion in the Alley Katz boutique and Yvonne Dunlop was killed. She was the mother of three little boys under nine, and had been minding the shop, which was owned by her own mother, as a favour.

In Long Kesh prison, Thomas McElwee became known for punching warders. He was six feet two. He appeared remarkably well during his hunger strike, and his death, which came on the sixty-first day, was sudden. Seamus Heaney, no supporter of the IRA, attended his wake as a neighbour, and later wrote about it in his poem 'The Wood Road'.

McElwee's funeral at St Mary's church in Bellaghy was a fraught one. Local people remember that the air was thick with helicopters. Pat Brennan, a native of Bellaghy who had returned from university in Britain that summer, tells me he was mesmerized by the television crews that had gathered to cover the funeral. He saw crews from Yugoslavia, Japan and China. He was shocked to see people he knew very well as moderate Catholics, 'educated people', now wearing black armbands in solidarity with the IRA hunger strikers. There were police vans everywhere and police in riot gear.

Many local people had gone to the church early in order to be sure of a seat. When the parish priest, Father Michael Flanagan, appealed for an end to the hunger strike, several women, including republican politician Bernadette McAliskey, walked out in protest. 'But a lot of local people were happy with what Father Flanagan said and believed he could have said a lot more,' says Pat Brennan now. 'They were very against people like them dying. They thought it was not a Christian thing or a Catholic thing to do.'

Two days after the McElwee funeral, there was a brawl at a local council meeting, featuring Oliver Hughes, a councillor who was a brother of Francis and a cousin of Tom McElwee. Oliver Hughes had demanded that the council meeting be adjourned, but unionist councillors were furious that it should be suspended in remembrance of a murderer. The chairman of the council got a nasty punch and the local MP, Willie McCrea of the Democratic Unionist Party, was taken into Magherafelt hospital in a wheelchair.

And now both the cousins lie under this polished black stone, with, on the day of our visit, a pot of marguerites and a red candle on top of them. The gravestone shows a Celtic female figure bent forward with a sword standing upright beside her. A wreath of green, white and orange artificial flowers lies on the grave, from Republican Sinn Féin, a splinter group that does not recognize the legitimacy of the Northern Irish state or peace process.

Another polished black grave in Bellaghy graveyard marks the final resting place of Mary McGlinchey, née O'Neil. Her grave has an upright stone depicting Cúchulainn fainting at his death pillar.

Mary McGlinchey was from Toomebridge, not far from Bellaghy, and was associated with many killings. Most of these seem to have taken place when her husband, Dominic McGlinchey, was in charge of the Irish National Liberation Army, the republican paramilitary group he had joined after breaking with the IRA. Mary McGlinchey was suspected of the killing of five INLA members during a feud within that organization. Her fingerprints were found at the scene of the murder of two RUC reserve constables, Snowden Corkey and Ronnie Irwin, at Markethill in County Armagh. She was also thought to have been involved in the death of another constable, Colin Carson, in May 1983.

She was killed at her home in Dundalk while she was bathing her two young sons. Her sons have subsequently said that she asked the gunmen to take her outside, but they ignored her request and shot her in the bathroom in front of her older son, Declan. The younger boy, Dominic McGlinchey Junior, was already in her bedroom, where she had been drying him and combing the water from his hair. 'They'd shot her that many times in the head,' Dominic Junior said many years later, 'that the back of her brains, all of that, was missing. Declan had put his hand into the back of her head and said, "Mammy, it's all right, you can get up now. The men are gone."' It was a Saturday night and the boys had been looking forward to the video van coming round so that they could hire a film for the evening. Their Saturday nights, Dominic Junior recalled, were once about 'the heat in the house and the smell of popcorn'.

Dominic McGlinchey, for his part, was another Bellaghy native. In a 1983 newspaper interview, he admitted to having killed about thirty people and to having been involved in the bombing of many small northern towns. 'I don't think a town wasn't blown up. They all got a touch – Kilrea, Bellaghy, Portglenone, Magherafelt, Maghera, Castledawson, Ballymena and a lot of others.'

McGlinchey was murdered by two republican gunmen in Drogheda as he left a telephone box. Dominic Junior, now aged sixteen, witnessed the murder. His father shouted to him to 'Run like fuck.' Dominic Senior was hit by fourteen bullets. Dominic Junior remembers 'the thickness of the blood. A real, real sticky tar-ness.'

Also buried in the local graveyard is Sean Brown, a school-teacher who was abducted while locking the gates of the local GAA club. His body was found beside a blazing car outside the neighbouring town of Toomebridge. His killers have never been found. The security cameras in Toome-bridge were discovered not to have been working on the night his body was dumped there. This was in 1996: late in the game. Heaney wrote a poem about the killing. Out of the order of his homeplace had come murder of the most intimate kind.

Dominic McGlinchey Senior was one of eleven children. Francis Hughes was the youngest boy in a family of ten. Thomas McElwee was one of twelve. Seamus Heaney was the oldest of nine. In this respect they came from another country: the country where Catholics did not use contra-ception and took babies as they came. The three IRA men are all buried in what is called the new graveyard of St Mary's church, which opened in 1981. Francis Hughes was the very first person to be buried there.

Seamus Heaney's grave is in the old St Mary's graveyard, across the road from the new one, under the sycamores beside the boundary ditch. The inscription on the sturdy and unvarnished vertical slab reads 'Walk on air against your better judgement', a line from one of his poems. He lies beside three Heaney family graves, separated from them by a little path. His grave is of the graveyard and of his ancestors, but in a place apart.

Father Andy Dolan lives at the opposite end of Bellaghy from the Seamus Heaney HomePlace, in the huge parochial house, which he thinks is too big. 'It was being built when I arrived here in the nineties,' he says, and he thinks its size could have been a statement about the growing strength of the Catholic community in Bellaghy. (Earlier he had told me, 'There's always someone pressing a wee button here, you know.')

There is a new sign, black lettering on a white background, outside the new graveyard now, directing people towards the graves of Francis Hughes and Thomas McElwee. It went up after the new sign in the old graveyard, black lettering on a white background, which directs people to Seamus Heaney's grave.

St Mary's Catholic church was built in the 1860s. Father Dolan is the only priest here now: 'I haven't had a curate now for a number of years.' When he was assigned the parish, he argued slightly with the bishop who had appointed him, because his predecessor, Father Flanagan, who had ministered at the Hughes and McElwee funerals, had been parish priest in Bellaghy for so long. No one could understand why he was being moved. Some parishioners protested, but Father Flanagan said that he had taken a vow of obedience, and left as the bishop had directed.

Father Dolan and I travel north out of Bellaghy to

Tamlaghtduff, the townland where the Hughes and McElwee families, and later the Heaney family, lived. A line of tightly sculpted copper beeches marks the beginning of Scribe Road. There is a plaque to the memory of Francis Hughes on the family home, which is now the centre of a steel construction business run by Francis's brother, Oliver. The firm has a good contract for providing the staircases for aeroplanes.

As we drive, our path is crossed by Ian Milne, once a member of the same IRA unit as Francis Hughes and Dominic McGlinchey: at one point they were described as the three most wanted men in Northern Ireland. He escaped from Portlaoise prison by helicopter, and later became a Sinn Féin representative on the Mid Ulster Council and an MLA at Stormont. He looks very normal.

There is money round here now. The cars are shiny. The houses are fine bungalows. We pass a large plot of land where a man is having an underground car park constructed for his collection of vintage cars. We pass a huge barn that has been converted into another property for Hughes Steel.

'The best thing that happened to the Catholics of Northern Ireland,' says Pat Brennan, was that Margaret Thatcher 'created an economy which suited the entrepreneurial spirit'.

The Protestant primary school here is down to thirty-five pupils. If it were to close, 'that would be a very bad day for this community', says Father Dolan. The local Catholic schools are thriving, with 220 pupils in St Mary's Primary and 150 in St John Bosco's.

It is in this context – of the ascendant Catholic community – that the Seamus Heaney HomePlace must be viewed. It is situated on the main street as you approach the town from the Magherafelt side, at the opposite end from St Mary's church and the parochial house. It is just up from the Poet's Corner café. As you drive out from Bellaghy towards Castle-dawson, where Seamus Heaney's mother was from and where there was once a Nestlé factory, you can see just how over-whelming the HomePlace is.

'It's very big and imposing, I know,' says Pat Brennan, who was instrumental in its creation. It is built on the site of the old RUC police station, which in its turn had been built on the site of an old house. Following the closure of the station, the Magherafelt council, dominated at that time by Sinn Féin, bought the site. But while they were delighted to have own-ership of an RUC station, 'They didn't have any real plans for it. There was a suggestion of a community centre,' says Pat.

At that time, a Seamus Heaney exhibition was housed in the Bawn, an old building that lies on the outskirts of Bel-laghy, just beyond the hairdresser's, Cuttin It Fine, and Fullerton's garage and Rainey's the bookie.

Pat Brennan, who retired early and returned to Bellaghy after a career in banking, had worked on Heaney's bibliog-raphy and compiled an inventory of the artefacts held at the Bawn. He had met Heaney in Dublin over the years and they would chat together about their hometown. 'I went to visit Marie Heaney one month after he died. She said that their house was coming down with books, and that she'd like his library to go to Bellaghy.' The Bawn, following the cutbacks after 2008, was open only one day a week. 'I came home and thought, it's wrong for the library to go to the Bawn.'

There was a plan forming.

'I first of all spoke to Ian Milne. I said, "You know the plans for the community centre? Would there be room for a library?" He stood back – like this is the best news he ever heard. Because they [Sinn Féin] wanted to demolish the RUC station.'

The site was on a hill, so there was plenty of room for expanding what had originally been envisaged as a single-storey community centre. They went back to the original architects and told them the new building would not be a community centre, but rather an interpretative centre dedicated to Seamus Heaney.

In the summer of 2018, Prince Charles visited the Heaney HomePlace. He is one of the celebrities reading Heaney poems on the interactive jukebox downstairs; he reads 'The Shipping Forecast'. Prince Charles is a big Heaney fan: 'He wrote a six-page letter to Marie Heaney when Seamus died.' He visited Bellaghy on an extraordinarily hot day. Local children performed extracts from *The Burial at Thebes*, Heaney's version of Sophocles' *Antigone*, a play about a king's refusal to bury a nephew who opposed him in war. Performing the extract was, Pat Brennan says, 'Here's two fingers up to you.' (This is a recurring theme in modern Irish nationalism: invite posh British people to your home and subject them to your version of history.) During the performance, a tin crown fell off a girl's head and rolled right to Prince Charles's feet. His wife, Camilla, Pat says, laughed a great deal.

Out past the turn for Castledawson is Mossbawn, Heaney's first home. Its land now is covered with chicken sheds, farmed by another family. In Heaney's youth, there was a railway line nearby, which facilitated the Nestlé factory and the other small industries that marked Northern Ireland's local towns. Only the chimney of the factory remains.

If you go down the Ballyscullion Road, you come to the GAA ground, with its one-storey clubhouse and its big sports hall. Over the entrance to the pitches an arch is filled with the iron letters declaring it 'Páirc Seán de Brún', after the man who was kidnapped from here as he locked the gates; he was murdered nearby.

As you return to Bellaghy, you pass a row of two-storey cottages with hanging baskets at the end of the road on the right. It was in the last of these cottages – painted white and pretty – that Dominic McGlinchey was born. His father, Gerald, was an alcoholic who drank away the garage he owned. Perhaps that is where Dominic McGlinchey's murderous rage came from, although who is to say?

Bellaghy was originally Vintnerstown, laid out as part of the plantation of Ulster. Many of the first Protestant settlers who came from Britain then went on to settle Pennsylvania.

At St Tida's Church of Ireland church, the stone drapery falls over the Junkin family plinth in the graveyard. The names here are Mawhinney, Overend, Davidson. There is the Downing vault, connected to the family after whom London's Downing Street was to be named. Inside the porch of the church, a line of six umbrellas, four short and foldable and two long and black, hang like staves. Even the bookcase is dedicated to the glory of God and in memory of Samuel (Sam) Overend, who died in April 2016. There is also a memorial to Private David McQuillan of the 5th County Londonderry Battalion of the Ulster Defence Regiment, 'Murdered by Terrorists, 15th March 1977. Aged 37.'

'He was waiting for a bus in the village to go to work,' says John Junkin, a tall, serious man with a strong interest in local history. David McQuillan's son was waiting for his school bus on the same street and witnessed the killing.

There are Presbyterians buried here too, and Bellaghy's First World War memorial is in the Presbyterian church, which lies between here and the road, and which also houses the majority of the memorials to Bellaghy people – policemen and members of the UDR – who were killed locally. But we can't get into the Presbyterian church, because its minister is very hard to get hold of – 'even if', as one Bellaghy person puts it, 'you're a Presbyterian'.

St Tida's church was built in 1620. It was burned in 1641 – the year of an Irish rebellion against England's rule and settlers – and again in 1740. It was rebuilt by 1792. The local clergyman and liberal John Hervey came in and saw the stone tower and gave £500 for the construction of a spire.

'We sold the rectory three or four years ago. We had no clergyman,' John Junkin says.

'I might be wrong, but it might just need one spark and it would be all the same again. There are ultranationalists here. They want to see me and anyone who's British out. If they won tomorrow, I'd be put to the sword.'

What can I say? I can't deny it. He knows more about this place than I do.

'I remember the 1956 Troubles – they blew up the phone box and wee bridges out round the country. Then things seemed to go quiet up till 1966' – the fiftieth anniversary of the Easter Rising, celebrated with much official fanfare in the Republic. 'That's when things began to hot up. The tricolours went up. I came back from Scotland because my mother and grandmother were being harassed.'

In 1981, John became a local Ulster Unionist Party councillor. In 1998, he was at Stormont as part of the UUP delegation, filling in for a colleague, as the negotiations for the Good Friday Agreement came to a climax. 'One of the members was called to a funeral and I was there on the final day of the Good Friday negotiations. I can still feel the heat of [the Agreement] in my hands off the photocopier. I arrived about eleven in the morning to the main building. They'd been talking all night. The party had warned them about doing that. The coffee machine ran out before ten the previous night.' He feels this was not the ideal setting for such weighty deliberations. 'In those circumstances I reckon those guys would sign their own granny's death warrant. David Trimble, Ken Maginnis – those boys like their steaks.'

John was firmly against the deal offered to unionists under the Good Friday Agreement. But he is not a fanatic. When I mention that local Catholics still speak of having been bullied by the B Specials, he says, 'It could have been true. The type of people who went to the B Specials – they favoured themselves.' But the old unionists in Stormont didn't see this.

'Sixty-two, sixty-three, sixty-four – they were idyllic times. I remember police came round on bicycles to see had we our weeds cut.' Looking back, this was when the unionists should have made concessions to the Catholic population, he says, but the opportunity was missed.

Then the violence came. Francis Hughes' life, John says, was saved by a Protestant nurse in Magherafelt hospital. 'The Spar shop was blown to pieces four times. Graham's. They still own it.'

His friend John McKay was almost murdered. 'But he saw the fishing line on his gate. It was one of the clothes-peg bombs. The filling station – it was a Protestant one at the time – was bombed.'

During the hunger strikes, 'everything closed down. You couldn't go riding on your bicycle.'

The Bellaghy shirt factory was burned. 'There were black flag protests on our road. It was very uncomfortable, very difficult.'

John remembers the punch-up at the Magherafelt council meeting very well. His wife was taking the minutes on the night. At another meeting, a child's coffin was brought in and kicked about.

'When Hughes had been buried, I thought, "How am I going to work this high wartime politics? We are chicken farmers at the end of the day." And I had to worry about Willie McCrea [long-time local MP of the more extreme Democratic Unionist Party]. So I went and bought myself an Amstrad computer and entered politics.'

Politics hasn't gone very well for the UUP since then,

with the DUP becoming the dominant force in unionism just as Sinn Féin has become the dominant force in nationalism. 'As I said to my wife: it's all come to nothing. We'd be better in Scotland with me the manager of a sheep farm.'

St Tida's has had a facelift since the opening of the Heaney centre, which is on the opposite side of the road. The Home-Place has brought more public spending on historic buildings in Bellaghy. But the community centre is out at St Mary's Catholic church, and 'Protestants won't use it', John says. There's also the GAA hall, which they won't use either.

According to John, there are only eight Protestants living in the town of Bellaghy now. The rest of them, he says, 'were intimidated out'.

Protestants, he says, 'don't like the Heaney centre. They wouldn't go out of their way to go there. It's not regarded as their thing. What Heaney said about the B Specials and about having never lifted a glass to the Queen. The Heaney centre is Roman Catholic. The Young at Heart Club meets in our parish hall – it has Presbyterians and Roman Catholics.'

And so we go for lunch in the Heaney HomePlace. I can see a couple of heads turn as we take our seats at the table by the door. They are surprised to see John Junkin there.

The Grave of Patrick Kavanagh and Katherine Barry Moloney

Not far from the Heaney HomePlace – just an hour's drive – is the homeplace of another poet. Patrick Kavanagh was the son of another small farm, of another family made up of nine children. He too grew up near a railway line, this one running between Dundalk and Carrickmacross. He became the leading Irish poet of his day, but whereas Heaney was an exemplary citizen who attracted love and honour around the globe, Kavanagh was often at odds with the world. And the strife did not end with his death.

In the sleepy village of Inniskeen, County Monaghan, the Kavanagh exhibition is a modest affair, housed in an old Protestant church and staffed by local volunteers who have kept the flame flickering for twenty-five years and who at the time of writing were waiting for money from Monaghan county council for a new Kavanagh centre, to be built in the grounds of the old Catholic church.

In June 2019, when I visit Inniskeen, Patrick Kavanagh's grave is a ruin: overgrown with weeds, its rear margin completely gone, only a small teak cross marking the resting place of one of Ireland's most famous poets.

Patrick Kavanagh was rarely grateful. Or tactful. His life was punctuated by rows, feuds and even a famous court case. His father, James, had also appeared in court and had a reputation amongst his neighbours as being knowledgeable about the law. 'I never belonged there. Terrible, ignorant, vulgar place Inniskeen,' wrote Patrick in a letter to his brother.

Kavanagh lived the last quarter-century of his life in the vicinity of Baggot Street and the Grand Canal in Dublin, a city he described, in a letter to his brother, as an 'illiterate and malignant wilderness'. As time passed, he drank more and more. My mother and her friends, young women in the Dublin of the 1950s, thought him a bit creepy.

He died at the end of November 1967, and his body was brought back to Inniskeen for burial, on 2 December, in torrential rain. The funeral procession was said to have been a mile long. His brother Peter, who was a good designer, planned the grave with careful attention, and carved the teak cross. The grave was laid with fourteen carefully chosen stones from the family homestead and the little farm Patrick's parents, with considerable financial effort, had bought for him in his youth. It was about this second farm that Kavanagh wrote his masterpiece *The Great Hunger*, about the celibate life of a single farmer, living within 'this apocalypse of clay'.

A few months before Kavanagh died, he had married Katherine (Kitty) Barry Moloney. Peter Kavanagh had not approved of the marriage: 'He married his drinking companion,' he wrote dismissively. Peter had not actually met Kitty when he wrote those words; they met for the first time at Patrick's funeral, when he was inviting rain-soaked mourners who were sheltering in a pub back to the Kavanagh house for refreshments. (Patrick Kavanagh had died owing £14 to the local publican in Inniskeen, Dan McNello.)

According to Peter, in his book *Patrick Kavanagh: A Life Chronicle*, Kitty grabbed his arm aggressively and shouted: '"Am I not being invited? I am Paddy's wife." The use of the undignified word "Paddy", never used in our family, riled me but I held my temper, fearing a rabbit punch or worse from my assailant.' Peter hated Kitty with an irrational passion – and there is no evidence that he had any reason to fear violence from her.

Having first met in artistic circles in London, Patrick and Kitty had been living together on and off for years. Some of Patrick's letters from London are from 47 Gibson Square, where Kitty had her flat. In one of these letters, dated 8 January 1964, he wrote to Peter: 'PS This address will get me even if I'm in Ireland.' So their relationship was far from casual. But Kitty's nephew, Eunan O'Halpin, told me that her family were insulted that it was portrayed in print by Peter Kavanagh 'as if Patrick was an oil tycoon and she was a hat-check girl'.

Peter, the youngest in the Kavanagh family, had devoted much of his early life to Patrick, who was twelve years older, and had supported him financially for years. Their relationship, on Peter's side at least, was fanatically close. In another letter addressed to Peter from Kitty's London flat, Patrick wrote: 'You are inclined to intrude on one's private world and use information acquired as a brother. Think of me as an acquaintance. It is hard to explain this but I know you are smart and get the idea.'

Peter shot back: 'If you were only an acquaintance I would not have put up with you for so long. I wish you were an acquaintance; it would solve the problem easily. But I am stuck with the relationship.'

In another of his books about Patrick, *Sacred Keeper*, Peter recounts how he felt on seeing his brother recuperating in a Dublin hospital after having a cancerous lung removed in 1955: 'This noble body, the object of all my affection and admiration – wrecked!'

This is not the sort of fraternal feeling commonly expressed between Irish brothers.

In Peter's eyes, perhaps, he and Patrick were a team, taking on the snobbery of a stupidly bourgeois world, fighting for its respect. Against this backdrop, Patrick's marriage seemed a betrayal. Patrick did not tell members of his family about the engagement, and Peter had learned of it through a third party.

Katherine Barry Moloney had worked as a bookkeeper in London and later in Dublin, and in both places she was part of a bohemian set, steady drinkers and heroic smokers, whose artist members were remarkable for their poverty. She was a niece of Kevin Barry, one of the martyrs of the Easter Rising in 1916, a medical student who was shot by the British and commemorated in a song so famous that it has now become a sort of cliché.

Upon her death in 1989, the rights to Patrick's work passed into the control of the board of trustees that had been operating the Kavanagh estate since Patrick's death. 'Not a Kavanagh among them!' Peter complained.

Hearing of Kitty's death at his home in New York, Peter wrote to tell her family that he would consider any opening of Patrick's grave in order to facilitate her burial there 'a desecration'.

There was negotiation with Patrick's sisters, who lived in Inniskeen, about the opening of one of their grave plots instead. When the time came for Kitty's coffin to be interred, the gravediggers refused to open the poet's grave to admit it. The funeral party had to adjourn to the nearby community hall while more discussions took place. Kitty's lawyer, John Jay, was at the funeral and had brought her will with him. In it she had specified that she wanted to be buried with her husband.

'Always bring the will to the funeral,' John Jay said to Eunan O'Halpin.

In the end, one of Kitty's colleagues from her job in Dublin, Sean Crowley, who was from Monaghan, dug into Patrick's grave with some other local men so that her coffin could be admitted.

According to Peter Kavanagh, he was kept informed of these events by Inniskeen people who resented the interference from 'the Dublin crowd'.

Of course a new burial in an existing grave disturbs it, and when Peter arrived back at Inniskeen later that summer, he writes, 'The memorial that had taken me years to develop was scattered, the grave in disarray, the cross broken.'

Kitty's sister, the artist Helen Moloney, designed a modernist gravestone, with a space carved through it 'like a scooped-out eyeball'. It was made by Tom Glennon of Deansgrange in Dublin. 'It had a very nice Roman lettering,' remembers Eunan O'Halpin. The stone was duly erected over Patrick and Kitty's joint grave.

In the summer of 1998, nine years after Kitty's death, the Moloney family got a phone call telling them that the grave had been vandalized and the gravestone destroyed. The stone pieces had been found in bogland near the Kavanagh farm. Eunan O'Halpin drove to Inniskeen that evening to find that the remains of the gravestone had been gathered into a trailer, a mess of fractured blocks. 'I took most of it home in big Superquinn bags.'

There had been an argument put forward – via the priest, but one senses the hand of Peter Kavanagh – that the new gravestone was inappropriate because it did not display a Christian image. In fact, Eunan O'Halpin says, there was a Maltese cross on the stone that measured about eight or nine inches. Surveying the ruins of the gravestone in the trailer, he spotted the cross: 'I made the parish priest come and see the cross, and he said nothing.'

Eunan left the fragments of the gravestone in the back garden of his house in Dublin. He subsequently moved out of the house, but as far as he knows, they are still there. Even now, the destruction of the stone seems vicious and pointless. 'It was upsetting for my aunt and for my mother,' he says.

Back in Monaghan, the local police had found the substantial sledgehammer that had been used to destroy the gravestone, and Peter Kavanagh, who was home from America, was questioned at the police station. But the police said they did not have enough evidence to press charges. Later, Peter freely admitted that he had been responsible. In *Patrick Kavanagh: A Life Chronicle*, he wrote: 'Eight years later, on August 11th 1998, I myself removed it and replaced it with the original memorial. So close to the surface was the widow buried that when replacing it there was a strong odour of sulphur.'

Peter's implacable hatred of his sister-in-law was perhaps partially motivated by the fact that the rights to Patrick's work had been left to her alone. Eunan O'Halpin says that

Peter, having provided financial support to Patrick over the years, had been relying on the rights to provide for him upon his own retirement. But even allowing for this disappointment, the extent of his malice is hard to fathom.

Peter Kavanagh had form in the matter of the destruction of memorials to his brother.

'In March 1973, my attention was drawn to a plaque erected outside The Plough pub in Soho,' he wrote. 'This plaque had been put up by some of Patrick's friends in London and its inscription, in Irish, read "*Is soma steall do chaith se anseo*" ("It is many a time he pissed here").'

The Kavanagh parents had not spoken Irish and this inscription was, bizarrely, translated by IRA prisoners in the maximum-security prison on the Isle of Wight, amongst whom one of Kavanagh's sisters, Celia, was working as part of her duties as a nun in the order of the Presentation of Our Lady at Matlock. (The Kavanagh family does not seem to have been remotely republican, and Kitty's republican family and left-wing politics were among the things Peter held against her.)

In any event, on learning the true meaning of the inscription on the Soho plaque, both Celia and Peter found it disrespectful.

'On December 27th 1973, accompanied by my two children and carrying tools adequate to destroy a plaque made of bronze and aluminium, I flew to London and tore it down in the middle of the day. This took no more than thirty seconds for the plaque turned out to have been made of plastic.'

Drinkers in The Plough came out to remonstrate, 'But recognizing me they retreated. I did not say a word.'

What made this talented, handsome man so furious, bitter and full of hate? His wife, Ann Keeley Kavanagh, remembered what she called Patrick's apt description of Peter as 'a rolling ball of emotion'. In writing about his childhood in Inniskeen, Peter said, 'There was a sense of community but irreconcilable feuds of several generations divided certain neighbours.' During a row he had with a neighbour as a boy, the neighbour shouted at him because their father, James, had been born out of wedlock: 'Get off my property, you bastard and the sons of bastards.' But such is village life in most places. Perhaps Peter drew closer to his own motivations when he wrote, 'No slight in Ireland, however deserved, is ever forgiven. The Irish ethic is a negative one – never to forgive.'

In September 2019, when I visited Inniskeen again, Patrick and Kitty's grave had been tidied and planted. But there was still no mention of Kitty Barry Moloney on the stone, nor did her name appear in the register of graves at the church. So in this if in nothing else, Peter Kavanagh can be said to have got what he wanted.

The Grave of Brendan Smyth

Brendan Smyth, a priest of the Norbertine order who died in August 1997 at the age of seventy, was buried at 4.15 in the morning. It is said that concrete was poured on his grave to prevent its subsequent desecration.

I had expected that the grave of arguably Ireland's most notorious paedophile would be hidden in some obscure corner of his former monastery, Kilnacrott Abbey in County Cavan. I walked through the grounds, fully expecting to be stopped as a trespasser at any moment. The graveyard for the Norbertine priests and brothers who once lived here lies on an open slope near the driveway that once led to the Norbertines' school. I was surprised to find that the little gate in the low fence was open. Then I realized that the graveyard itself is quite open, on the side that faces the entrance gates to the property, which was sold when the Norbertines fled Ireland. Their last Mass was said here on 24 September 2016.

As you enter the graveyard through the little gate, there is a memorial to a Smith just in front of you, on the right-hand side. But this is the grave of Mattheus Smith, 'born 21st October 1858, ordained 19th March 1881 and died 4th February 1940'. It is the first in a line of a dozen Norbertine graves, and one of only two inscribed in Latin. The hand of Vatican II fell on this graveyard when a Father Connell died on Christmas Eve 1968 and was given a gravestone written in English. On the left-hand side, Brendan G. Smyth's grave is one of four. He seems to have been buried with all the conventions granted to other priests. But one of his victims campaigned to have the title 'Reverend' removed from the stone, which now says simply 'Brendan G. Smyth O. Praem 1927–1997. Rest In Peace'.

Brendan Smyth was born John Gerard Smyth in Belfast; he was given the name Brendan when he entered the

Norbertine order. He died in his sleep at the Curragh prison, one month into a twelve-year sentence. (He had already served a sentence in Northern Ireland.) He was convicted of 117 cases of indecent assault on 41 children in the North and the Republic. There were 74 convictions for indecent assault of 20 children in the Republic between 1967 and 1993, and 43 convictions for indecent assault of 21 children in Northern Ireland between 1964 and 1984. In 1994, the Irish attorney general's mishandling of an extradition request from Northern Ireland led to the fall of the government.

Smyth also abused children during a period working in the United States. The extent and geographical scope of his crimes was possible only because the Norbertines and Church officials, when made aware of allegations against him, moved him from parish to parish rather than report the allegations to the police.

The man who would later become Cardinal Sean Brady held secret canonical investigations into Smyth's abuse of two boys in 1975. Even Smyth's ordination by Archbishop John Charles McQuaid in 1951 took place despite what the Northern Ireland Historical Abuse Inquiry called 'a clear warning from the [Norbertine] Abbot General'. In the 1940s, Smyth had been sent to study in Rome and returned under a cloud, and it was rumoured even amongst the Norbertine community in Cavan that this was the result of 'an incident with a child', according to his consistent critic within the Norbertines, Father Bruno Mulvihill. The Norbertines at Kilnacrott were later revealed to have resented what they saw as interference in their affairs from another branch of their order. Father Mulvihill stated that over the years, he had warned his local bishop, the Papal Nuncio of the time, two Norbertine abbots at Kilnacrott and, in 1986, the Norbertine abbot general in Belgium about Smyth.

I shove my hand into the gravel covering the grave of Brendan Smyth and find concrete lying beneath it. But there also seems to be concrete under the gravel on the other three graves beside his, and also on the twelve graves opposite. What is striking is how pristine the graves are.

The back avenue is lined with dark conifers, now too close together. There are no birds. Everything in this section of the property feels abandoned. There are walled enclosures with no gardens within them, and the willowherb stands five or six feet high. Withered blackberries are dying where they hang. But things pick up as you approach the back of the original Victorian house. This is now the home of the Cavan Centre, a registered charity that describes itself as a 'residential centre for education and community development'. There is a sandpit, and plastic tanks for the harvesting of rainwater. An old chimney, perhaps once part of a laundry, is painted red and white. There is a litter bin in the Gothic portico at the front of the old house, with its carefully studded door.

As I leave, about ten young people are being hoisted, one or two at a time, onto the high frame of an adventure climbing apparatus. They are wearing helmets with their harnesses, to protect them from harm.

One Sunday in January 2019, Keith Brady sent me a photograph of a strong arm sending a parabola of ashes out over the edge of a stone bridge, across a flat pond. Two skyscrapers stood in the background, behind bare trees. 'Mum made it to New York,' said the message. 'Hope you're keeping well. Keith xx'

Jennifer and Keith had always planned to take Bernie to New York for her sixtieth birthday. In the year before her death, they thought she was a year older than she actually was – fifty-nine rather than fifty-eight, and they had secretly phoned up her bosses at Marks & Spencer to make sure that she could take time off work. 'Then she got sick,' says Keith. 'And then she passed away.'

So he and Jennifer and Jennifer's friends Louise and Fiona decided to go to New York anyway, to mark her birthday.

'And she went with us,' Keith tells me when we meet. 'We had her in a shot glass, we had her in a lunch box – and in this.' He touches the silver vial that hangs around his neck, slim against his huge frame. The vial contains some of Bernie's ashes. She is with Keith all the time.

It was lashing rain on 24 January, Bernie's birthday. So they went to Central Park the following day, when the weather was fine. The girls had already been shopping at an outlet park in New Jersey – Keith had been sent back to the hotel with the first instalment of their innumerable shopping bags. Very much his mother's son, he says they got good value: 'Fiona got two Michael Kors bags and a Michael Kors wallet all for under five hundred dollars.' They had walked around Manhattan and had a very good time.

At the lake in Central Park, Jenny handed Keith the shot glass with a portion of Bernie's ashes.

'And I gave it a good throw, straight out into the water. That was it, she was gone.'

We look at the photo again, with the ashes arching out over the water like, as Keith says, a feather.

'I'd learned my lesson from when we scattered her ashes over the lake in Blessington,' he says.

Blessington reservoir in County Wicklow was one of Bernie's favourite places to walk.

'I thought it would be like in the movies and the ashes would scatter very finely. But they just went plop, straight into the water. Me and Jennifer broke our shites laughing. So I knew this time to give them a good throw.'

There's a photo of the shot glass containing Bernie's ashes. It is a small jar with a screw top and a handle. We look at photos of Central Park in January.

'So that's the view my mam had. She would have loved it and stayed there taking photos. It was strange, because afterwards birds started coming up to us because they thought we were throwing food.'

During that trip, Keith felt that Bernie was very close to them. 'It's mad. Even packing your bag, I could imagine her excitement at going over there, like a kid at Christmas, and her going shopping and walking and taking photos all the time. When we arrived, we were too early to check into the hotel so we went to the pub and Jenny said, "I feel like phoning Ma and telling her we've arrived safely." And I said, "She's here – in a suitcase back at the hotel."'

For Keith, the trip was another milestone in his grief.

'What I remember about grief is, in the early stages it's hard to recall the good times. That's what I found at first. You could see just a few memories. For example, she used to make an Irish stew – her way – and I got the recipe before she passed away and I made it but it wasn't the same. But now I make it in a proper pan and the smell of it, the taste of it, it makes the house sort of warm again.'

It is eighteen months since Bernie's death, and Keith feels that he has changed.

'I've grown up. I don't know, you see the world different. I remember looking at people on Facebook and they're moaning about their little complaints and I was talking to Jenny about it. You just feel like saying, "Would you ever fuck off and cop on? Look out for yourself and don't take any crap."'

They spent Christmas at their father's house for the first time ever: Jenny, Keith, Jenny's partner and the children.

They went to the hospice's Light Up My Life day at Christmas. They stood in the garden outside what had been Bernie's room for so long. The blinds were open, 'And inside was just a desk and two chairs. They've closed that ward and moved all the people into the new wing. It's an interview room now.'

Keith wants to know if I've been back to the hospice. I tell him no: Bernie's death took more out of me than I appreciated at the time. It's strange, I say, when I have written about some very tough things, that it affected me so deeply.

'But you'd never met anyone like my ma,' says Keith.

And it's true, I never had.

I O

Dermot Hourihane

14 July 2020

The phone rings at 2.50 in the morning, but I miss it. In the deepest of sleeps after a restless night, my brain can't recognize the noise.

At 2.52, the phone rings again. I think of the old Ry Cooder song 'Trouble, You Can't Fool Me'. Trouble is no longer hiding behind that tree; it's here on my bedside table. Trouble right here in River City, my father would say.

The second time, I manage to answer. It is the night nurse at my father's nursing home. He is having difficulty breathing, she says. His oxygen levels are dropping. Should she call an ambulance? My father told her, she says, that she should call an ambulance because he couldn't breathe. Well, I say, if she thought she should call an ambulance and my father thought she should call an ambulance, then she should call an ambulance. I will go to the nursing home and then travel with him to the hospital.

The hospital. The hospital. The hospital where my father had spent four miserable weeks, and from which he'd been discharged only a week earlier. At first, because of the COVID regulations, he was unable to receive visitors in any form, but eventually we were able to visit him a couple of times a week in the atrium of the hospital reception area. Between his mask and the effects of Parkinson's disease, we couldn't hear what he was saying. He who was once the loudest person anybody knew.

Parkinson's doesn't kill you, the consultant had told me on our first visit to him. People with Parkinson's die of something else, like pneumonia or perhaps a fall.

The hospital where in that same reception area we had told him he couldn't come home. That we were looking for a really nice nursing home. He said okay. I said that I'd found a newly built place but that I had problems with the design: it was like a golf club, I said. Great, said my father, who loved golf clubs.

He had agreed to go into the nursing home. The only stipulation he made was that he wanted a room that looked out onto a garden. We didn't realize then that because he was entering the nursing home from a general hospital, he would have to be quarantined for fourteen days. We could visit him through a window. He would be alone in his very nice room with just the carers for company.

Things started well. After a month of physiotherapy in the hospital, he was standing, and even walking a little. He stood up when the woman who was in charge of his floor entered the room.

'Ah,' she said. 'A gentleman.'

'I used to be a gentleman,' he said.

'And tall,' she said.

'I used to be five foot eleven,' he said.

Then he had lunch, and even ate pudding. He was so thin

that his wrists looked like those of a sensitive teenage girl. He had a glass of the wine I had brought him, even though it was not chilled.

'I haven't had a drink for four weeks,' he said.

'How was your pudding, Dad?' I said.

'Ephemeral,' he said.

I got Lyric radio for him on his huge television and he drifted off to sleep on the bed as I watched.

That night he fell. The next morning, he fell again. He was taken to hospital by ambulance. I sat in accident and emergency and read a book.

My father had broken his hip. Not a bad break, the surgeon said on the phone, but he'd need an operation.

Six days later, he was discharged: back to the nursing home, and to a new room. He had described the garden as 'without imagination' and had been transferred to a nicer room on the other side of the building, overlooking a path and some trees. He was in quarantine again.

We visited him through the window, but the stout windows of the newly built nursing home did not open fully, and again it was difficult to hear him. It was a wet week. My mother stood under an umbrella and they touched hands through the window.

The day before the phone call in the middle of the night, I had visited my father. I had grabbed the television remote through the window and concentrated on flicking channels to get him the cricket, or reruns of past Wimbledon finals. Only seven days of quarantine left, Dad, I said. He looked despairing. You must think of Burt Lancaster in *Birdman of*

Alcatraz, I said. Mum is coming tomorrow. I'll see you over the weekend.

So, now the phone call has come. I remember my phone charger. I run two red lights on the deserted road to the nursing home and get there in twelve minutes. Rina, who phoned me, and Jay, who I think is a care assistant, are waiting for me. They both look worried. The ambulance is already outside. The ambulance people are with him, Rina says. I can't go in to be with my father in his room, because of the COVID restrictions.

Jay is a young black Irish guy who looks like a rugby player. 'I talk about rugby with your father,' he says.

I go outside.

I go back inside.

I don't know where I go.

The female ambulance person comes out. Can I go with my father in the ambulance? I ask.

No, she says, due to the COVID restrictions.

They bring my father out of the nursing home on a sort of stretcher trolley.

'Dad, Dad,' I say. 'It's me.'

'He's unresponsive,' Rina says.

His eyes are half closed.

They put him in the ambulance. I say I will drive to the hospital and meet them there. 'By the way,' I say, 'do you know he has a non-resuscitation order in place?'

'There's nothing about that here,' says the female ambulance person, looking at the papers in her hand.

'Well, his GP has a copy and his consultant at the hospital has a copy,' I say. I name both the doctors.

I drive quickly to the hospital, leaving before the ambulance, which never appears in my rear-view mirror.

The ambulance arrives at the hospital five or ten minutes after me. My father's clothing has been pulled back, his chest is bare and his breathing is upside down. His stomach rises and falls at the wrong time. I take his hand.

I go to the accident and emergency waiting room and register him. They have his details already.

I plug in my phone charger and wonder what to do. I can't phone people at this hour.

I phone my brother. He says he's coming.

About ten minutes later, a doctor comes out of A&E and talks to me at its entrance. She is kind behind her mask. My father is very ill, she says. He is displaying a type of skin mottling. They have given him morphine and a drug to help his breathing.

Should I call the family? I say.

Yes, she says.

But it's ten to four in the morning, I say, like a fucking eejit.

Call them, she says. We could lose him tonight.

I phone my brother again. He's on his way. He will collect my mother, he says.

My father is not known or even suspected to have COVID, but because he is coming from a nursing home, the hospital works on the assumption that he has it, and so he is in the

A&E COVID room. And because the pandemic is in a lull at the moment – it's July 2020 – the room is otherwise empty. I am allowed to gown up and go in with him. I'm not sure if this is because there are no other patients, or because my father is dying, or both.

The nurse, Anne, is strict. My hair is stuffed into a blue cap. Now I look like a nurse, or a doctor.

My father is lying in a curtained cubicle under fluorescent lighting.

His breathing is terrible. Each inhalation sounds like the crackle of stones on a beach after a wave is sucked back into the sea. Crackle, crackle, crackle.

Or rattle, rattle, rattle.

When my sister and I were very young and shooting each other and pretending to die – I loved pretending to die, pretending to say your final words, pretending you couldn't hear the voices of your loving comrades – my father wasn't impressed. That isn't how people die at all, he said. Then he'd lie down on the couch and his lower jaw would go in and out. And then his breath would stop. I personally didn't appreciate this realistic depiction of death. It lacked glamour and I hadn't seen it exemplified by my heroes – you think the Little Match Girl looked that bad? – so I went back to trying to die with a bit of style.

But my father was correct in his mimicry. Back then, as a young pathologist in his twenties or thirties, he had been foreshadowing, with a good deal of accuracy, how he looks now in the resuscitation room.

'It's hard work, Dad,' I say. 'It's labour.'

During our childhood, my father used to bring home sections of cancerous lung or other organs, suspended in what seemed to be solidified jelly, and leave them on the kitchen dresser. He subscribed to a medical journal called *The Breast*, which proved to be much less exciting than it sounded to those of us who did not have breasts at the time. Don't look at that, he would say. There are things in it that might upset you. Once I saw a photograph of an amputated breast with a sore on it that appeared to be a second nipple.

My father would leave the house early to chair monthly 'death conferences'. At these meetings, the management of difficult cases was discussed after the completion of post-mortem examinations in a no-blame atmosphere that was unusual in medical culture at the time (and may be even rarer now). He sometimes put on a waistcoat to appear in court.

He had entered medical school at sixteen – 'too young' – and then went to London with his new wife, my mother, to train. He worked under Israel 'Sonny' Doniach, and Doniach was a big name in our early childhood: strange, but easy to say. It was under Doniach that my father did his work on how asbestos killed the men who worked with it by igniting a process within their lungs called mesothelioma. He worked with children who had leukaemia, many of whom died – and this was the only time, he said, when his work made him weep. It was while he was working at Hammersmith hospital that he fell ill with pneumonia – the twenty Player's untipped that he smoked each day cannot have helped – and I was brought to see him in hospital, with his bed tilted back so that his lungs could drain. The unnatural angle of the bed upset me, despite my father's jaunty wave.

He returned to Ireland to teach at Trinity College. We were told that he was a good teacher – although who is going to tell you that your father is a lousy teacher? He was one of the lecturers, most of whom were Catholic, who opposed the Archbishop of Dublin's ban on Catholics entering Trinity as undergraduates, on pain of being considered unworthy to receive the sacraments. (The archbishop's ban was lifted in 1970.) My father also became one of the founder members of the Irish Family Planning Association. Both of these campaigns and their attendant publicity caused consternation amongst his more conservative relatives. But the publicity did not bother him. We suspected that he rather liked it. 'The smell of the greasepaint . . .' my mother would mutter. But she supported him in these campaigns; they were a team.

He coordinated the merger of the pathology laboratories of the seven small independent Dublin hospitals, and piloted the opening of the central pathology laboratory at St James's hospital. All of this involved a great deal of medical politics. He would come back from committee meetings, having missed dinner with us, and talk about it in the kitchen with my mother as he ate. He wanted the separation of Church and state, he wanted an Irish laboratory service that was of international standard, and he wanted his dinner. He could be scathing, a formidable opponent with a needle of aggression that all his children inherited. He was a great heckler.

Much later, in old age, he would talk about his time in London as a postgraduate student, and how he had refused to make tea for the rest of the pathology team because it seemed subservient to him. He also talked about a doctor he had trained with. The two of them used to do the ward rounds together and see the patients, and the implication was that it was unusual for a pathologist to be taken on ward rounds. This man was very English and 'he always wore morning dress because he saw private patients in the afternoon'. My father did not have much time for this sort of thing. But he told a story about a patient they had met on the ward round who was dying – 'her eyes were rolling in her head' – and the man in morning dress got to the end of the ward round and said that he was going back in to be with this patient. 'I suppose it was because he had been in the war,' my father said. Later, when my father was applying for his job in Trinity, this man rang the university from London to say that my father was the best young pathologist he had ever worked with. No one told my father this at the time, and when he found out many years later, after the doctor's death, he regretted that he had never been able to thank him.

One of the male nurses starts to talk loudly in the silence of the resuscitation ward. I poke my head out of the curtains and put a finger up to my masked mouth.

Is there anything you would like? the nurses ask.

I say the lights are very bright. They try to dim them, but it doesn't make a lot of difference.

You're so thin, Dad, I say. Remember when you wanted

to be a serious rugby player and you couldn't, because you were so thin?

Mum is coming.

I have not shed a tear.

A young radiographer arrives with a portable X-ray machine. They want to take a chest X-ray, for diagnostic purposes. (My mother was a radiographer.) They lift the back of my father's bed. He is completely passive, whacked out of it on morphine, or perhaps simply dying. 'It's for diagnosis, Dad,' I say. He would like that.

I leave the cubicle for a minute, just to let the radiographer do her work. When I come back, my father looks worse. And quiet now: the rattle has stopped. But he is still breathing.

A male nurse comes in and looks at a monitor that is checking oxygen levels: little white mountains fill the screen: 72 over 107; 69 over 107.

'The family is coming?'

I say yes. (Where the hell are they?)

I stay with Dad. I hold his hand.

Someone brings tea with sugar and ginger biscuits. I eat them all.

Anne comes in to ask if my father is religious.

I smile and say, 'On the contrary.'

But my father was religious in his youth and as a young man. My earliest memories of church are of him showing me the illustrations in his missal. In our small Catholic community in London, altar boys were in short supply, and my father sometimes served Mass. Later I remember crying when he told me he didn't believe in God any more. I was a little convent girl and very religious. The Pope's encyclical prohibiting the use of contraception did it for him, I think. That came in 1968. I prayed hard for him then.

Now I leave the cubicle again to ring my brother. They're just at the hospital gate, he says.

When I go back to my father, he has turned to yellow wax. But breathing.

My brother and mother arrive, all gowned in blue. My mother looks very pretty. When we enter the cubicle, they gasp at the sight of him. This rugby player, this birdwatcher, this gardener, this golfer.

The radiographer arrives again: the battery in the machine had been flat for the previous X-ray, and they have to do it again. (Later, we will learn that the cause of my father's death was aspiration pneumonia, the most common cause of death in people with Parkinson's. It is caused by the failure of the swallowing reflex, which leads to them inhaling food or liquids into their lungs, which in turn leads to infection.)

I leave my mother and brother with my dad and go out to a small glass-walled office to phone my brother in Singapore. There's no reply.

The male nurse comes barrelling in to the small office to say that I must come now.

When I get to my father's bedside, I think he's dead already. I cannot see any sign that he is breathing – but he is. He is a yellow shell. His cheekbones are stark. He looks like an artistic representation of a saint.

A bit later, I leave his bedside for a phone call.

When I go back in, my mother is asking for his mouth to be closed.

I don't think I understood that my father was dead until Anne the nurse put a brace on his neck – in order to keep his mouth closed. That somehow made it clear to me that he was no longer in his body, which no longer looked like him.

We did not stay with the body any longer than ten minutes. All the information I'd picked up from him about the ways different communities kept vigil – the Greek Cypriots, the old Jewish ladies who were paid to sit beside the bodies of their dead in the morgue of the Royal London Hospital in Whitechapel, where my father worked for a while (the old ladies always fell asleep, he said) – was nothing to me now. Later, I was sorry that we had left so quickly.

We walked out into the daylight of a summer morning and went to our cars.

I reached my parents' house before the others. The burglar alarm was going off. I had to upend my handbag onto the floor of the hall to scrabble for my phone, which had the alarm code on it.

It wasn't yet 6 a.m.

This house was the scene of my father's decline. I could see him turning, turning, when turning took forever, to switch off a light. Or leaving his stick beside the sink when he went to wash his hands: a dangerous manoeuvre that sometimes resulted in one of his clattering, heart-stopping falls.

Or setting off without his stick to inspect his seedlings,

which were kept on the kitchen windowsill – 'I've discovered that germination is my strong suit.' This drove my mother crazy.

Or putting down his gardening tools and going back into the house, saying that he couldn't do this any more.

Or pricking out his seedlings at the kitchen table, leaning further and further to the right, almost to a forty-five-degree angle, and me trying to get him to come back to the perpendicular. This is known by Parkinson's specialists as Pisa syndrome.

Look, Dad, take this point on the window as your guiding line. I'm afraid you'll fall.

And then, after dinner, he leaned so far to the right that he did fall.

'Sorry, sorry,' he said.

And I said, 'Don't be sorry, Dad. Please don't be sorry.' Then I cried and put my arms around him, and he switched to parent mode – something he did very easily, taking charge: 'Sure we're all sorry.'

At the very beginning of the pandemic – in March when the nights were still dark, in April when the nights were still cold – my little car was often the only moving vehicle on the dual carriageway as I drove home from my parents' house. Sometimes there was a Garda checkpoint, and on the advice of a garda who had stopped me I kept one of my parents' utility bills in the glove compartment, to prove that I was a carer. I wondered how many other people were making journeys like these.

I was so alone on this normally busy road that it felt like

science fiction. This is how the pandemic changed the way we worry about the people we love, and grieve for them. It halted the daily life that ordinarily provides contrast and comfort to people who are losing, or have lost, someone; the activity that sustains the expression 'life goes on'. I was waiting patiently at traffic lights where there was no traffic. I was being overtaken by the blue lights of ambulances that had no need of their sirens. My father was still alive, and at home, but I knew that this eeriness was grief. I was a junior astronaut, alone in outer space.

Death was coming for my father for such a long time. His neurologist told me that many of his patients who had been diagnosed with Parkinson's after my father died long before him. It was my father's character, he said, that had kept him alive for so long.

Who can you call at such an early hour of the morning? I phoned the nursing home, and Rina told me that my father had squeezed her hand and said 'Thank you.' As far as I know, these were the last words he ever said.

We waited as long as we could to call others, but we were still phoning so early that everyone knew it must be bad news. Or 'sad news', as I called it. Or 'rather sad news', as my mother called it. It was strange to be saying 'Dad died this morning' over and over again, to so many people.

My brother took my mother to the supermarket – this just hours after she had lost her husband. She insisted on going. Half jokingly, half seriously, we tried to tell her she was breaking a social taboo: as a newly widowed person, she was supposed to be shrouded in the privacy of her own home. But the supermarket was her place of safety, and she knew she would need food for all the people who would be calling to the house in the next few days.

Our cousin Margaret, who does not cook, later dropped a bag containing two dishes of pasta with spinach and pine nuts, two beef lasagnes and a cake to our house. Every time we ate one of these dishes, my mother blessed Margaret's name.

While my brother and mother were at the supermarket, the doorbell rang. It was my aunt, with a large bunch of flowers. She is a recent widow and had been self-isolating for four months, because she has a respiratory disease. In all that time she had not called to anybody's house. We agreed that we would stand in the garden. I told her at some length about my father's death and how we were with him when he died.

'You were lucky,' she said.

And she told me of her husband's death in his nursing home, and how she had not been with him. I had not heard this story before, and I understood its significance in a way I would not have done even a day earlier, before my father died. I had joined a club, the club of people who have lost someone.

My father had not anticipated that his death would be marked with a funeral, having pledged his corpse to science back in the 1970s. If there is no body, there can be no funeral. We had discussed the possibility of a celebration of his life, to be held in Trinity College at a later date, and he had chosen some pieces of music to be played at it. But the donation-of-remains programme at Trinity, and similar schemes at other institutions, had been suspended since the start of the pandemic. So we had his body, and we had to organize a funeral he had never envisaged or wanted. I say we had to organize a funeral; it would be more accurate to say that it never occurred to us to do anything else. Equally, it never occurred to us to use the traditional Catholic ritual: we knew he didn't want that. So we had to be a bit creative.

Some decisions were easy. Cremation. A simple coffin – though not wicker, because I had gathered in my research for this book that some wicker coffins are problematic in cremations, failing to burn properly. My brother said that he always thought wicker coffins looked like laundry baskets. My mother didn't want a wicker coffin either, although she had previously declared that she would like to be buried in one herself. I thought pine. My brother thought oak. My mother liked oak. So we got a plain oak coffin with no brass fittings and no cross.

No flowers, except those from my parents' garden.

One car.

We were a funeral director's nightmare.

I wanted to read the Buddhist Metta Sutta, because it had always reminded me of our father – and maybe, in retrospect, also of the Our Father. I suggested to my brother that one of Dad's friends should do the eulogy, because he'd had so many friends and people would get sick of looking at relatives. We were making it up as we went along.

As a human gathering, the funeral was limited by COVID.

Attendance was capped at thirty-five people – more generous than at other stages of the pandemic, but restrictive enough to change the nature of the occasion. My sister, who lives in the UK, and my brother, who lives in Singapore, could not come back to Ireland. This was very hard for them, and also for us. We felt that half our family was missing, yet somehow hovering – as if the three absentees might walk in at any moment and stand over us, giving their opinions on our plans.

We could not reach one of my father's most faithful friends, a newer friend whom he had met at his golf club and whom none of the rest of us knew. We tried ringing the club, but its offices were closed for the weekend. We tried looking him up in the phone book, but we did not know how to spell his name. This was the man who had rung my father regularly in the months when he had been housebound, who dropped bottles of wine to his doorstep. There are limits to social friendships, and a long-term debilitating illness tends to expose them. In Ireland, we are often relieved – I know I have been relieved – to leave the sick person to the private care of the family (usually to the women of that family) and not get in touch. I believe this is particularly the case for friendships between men. But my father's friend from the golf club stayed in touch to the end.

Even as we were organizing the funeral, we did not know when it would take place. There was no word on when my father's body would be released to the undertaker. When we put the death notice on RIP.ie, we had to end it by saying 'details to follow'.

On the night after my father's death, my brother and I stayed in my parents' house. I went to bed dreading waking up the next day, to a world without my father. But in the morning, I was fine.

My mother and I had to decide what to wear to the funeral, and also what my father would wear in the coffin. In the end, we decided that he would wear a sports coat and a shirt with a tie, which was what he had worn in his working life. My brother brought these clothes to the undertakers and brought back my father's shoes. You don't wear shoes if you are being cremated. These small, sharp facts come frequently after a death, and you absorb them almost without pain.

At a quarter past two that afternoon, I brought an old pair of my mother's sandals to the shoemaker. It was a Saturday. My father died yesterday, I said, and I know you don't open on Monday, so you have to fix these for me now, because I'm wearing them to the funeral. I'm going to pretend they are fashionable slides. The shoemaker smiled at this, because he knew what a vain hope it was. He said he was sorry my father had died and that he closed on Saturdays at three o'clock. If I came back in half an hour, he would have them ready for me.

I took a phone call from my Australian cousin who lives in London. I went to Lidl and bought a large box of masks for giving out to anybody who might need one. I phoned my sister. I picked up the sandals from the shoemaker, who said that all he had been able to do was put on a temporary patch. They would not last long, he said, pointing out their numerous vulnerabilities. It was touch and go with the sandals.

Then I got on a bus and went into town to queue outside clothes shops. My mother needed good tights and I needed . . . everything. It was hot. I was sweating. And I was not allowed to try anything on. The girl in the tights department of Brown Thomas said that older ladies usually preferred a finer denier. We agreed that this was because the finer tights reminded them of the glamorous nylon stockings of their youth.

I brought everything back to my house. I felt that my father was still with me.

Each time I went to my parents' house, there was a new list of things to do, and new things achieved. We had only half an hour for the entire ceremony, and the programme was filling up. The grandchildren were to do readings: my mother's favourite prayer and a poem. The grandchild in Singapore was writing a poem. Our brother in Singapore was writing his reflections.

My brother was organizing everything. There was a sense that I, being the only sibling in Dublin, had been in charge while my father was alive, and my brother was in charge of him now that he was dead. The only thing we disagreed on was the matter of carrying the coffin.

To be invited to carry a coffin is an honour, but the practice is not universal. It has generally not been done within my (urban, bourgeois) family. When my father attended his aunt's funeral in Northern Ireland, he was asked to carry the coffin. 'Like the bloody IRA,' he said, although of course he did it.

My mother's brother, on the other hand, was very fond of the coffin being carried. After the funeral of a family friend, he remarked approvingly: 'That's the advantage of having five sons.' He had four himself. After the funeral, as we walked up the hill to the car, you could see him counting his treasure.

Carrying the coffin is almost always a male prerogative, but my brother didn't want to do it. He suggested that I do it instead. I thought this would look stagey and self-conscious, and I didn't have the energy to make a statement. (Here, again, the IRA comes to mind. Women carried the coffin of the IRA operative Mairéad Farrell, who was shot by the SAS while on a bombing mission in Gibraltar in 1988. In one of the photos of the funeral, I thought I saw an old friend from university under the coffin. You could tell her by the curl of her dark hair against the wood.)

We could get the male cousins to do it, I said. No, said my brother, if the cousins carried the coffin, everyone would wonder why he wasn't doing it.

I was worried that my brother would become too stressed. For this reason I suggested that we employ a humanist celebrant for the funeral. Someone who knew the form and could shape the thing, instead of us having to do it all.

It turned out that we were a humanist celebrant's nightmare as well. When the celebrant called to the house to discuss arrangements, he told us that at funerals he usually explained something about humanist philosophy. 'No, no, no,' I said. 'Show, don't tell.'

Then he said he usually walked up the aisle at the start of the funeral, in front of the coffin.

'No,' said my mother, who had been very quiet. 'Just the family.'

It took some time to persuade the humanist celebrant to stay.

I went back to my house then and a friend called round, bringing enough food to keep me for four days. And also approving the top I had bought for the funeral.

I sat down to select the music. This proved much more difficult than I had expected. For example, when we had discussed the anticipated memorial service, my father had told me he wanted the quartet from *Fidelio*. But it turned out there are at least three quartets in *Fidelio*. Who knew? I reckoned it had to be 'Mir ist so wunderbar' from Act One. Which, it turns out, is so beautiful that it made me cry. Another of his choices was the Lacrimosa from Verdi's Requiem – which he used to sing while he was shaving, my mother told me. None of his children inherited his passion for classical music. He said we were savages. But as he got sicker, I used to bring him to cinema screenings of operas. After listening to 'Mir ist so wunderbar' I was going to say to him, 'I get it now, Dad.' But it was too late.

I had to phone a friend to ask which recordings were best – Jessye Norman with the Staatskapelle Dresden for the *Fidelio* quartet, he said. Then we had to enlist a grandchild to send the links. That was on Monday, the day before the funeral.

My brother said that due to the COVID regulations, no one was allowed to carry the coffin up the aisle, because it broke the rules of social distancing.

By now I felt like some sort of mad theatrical impresario in full spate. On my way into town to bring the rejected items back to the shops, I had had to get off the tram to take a phone call from my nephew in Singapore and tell him that I was cutting his poem – eighteen lines long – in half. Then I rang my brother in Singapore to tell him that his reflections on my father could not be included, as they were so personal that they could only be delivered by him. This, combined with the fact that he could not be in Ireland for the funeral, hurt him dreadfully. I blush to think of it now.

Later on, having calmed down, I enlisted a cousin to read my brother's reflections. My nephew's poem remained halved, and so did the Metta Sutta.

On the morning of the funeral, I had to drive back to my own house to get a locket, because my mother said that I needed something around my neck. She looked calm; in fact, beautiful.

The funeral car arrived early at my parents' house. There was a tube of something in the middle of the back seat. The driver, who was very kind, said, 'There's hand sanitizers there for all of youse and you can keep them. Very welcome.' We went to the morgue at the hospital, and saw the bare coffin, on its own in a windowless room. I think those of us who had witnessed my father's death – my mother, my brother and myself – were sort of inured to it by that time. But my nephew, the youngest of his family, got a terrible shock when he saw the closed coffin so naked before us. Poor boy.

What could we do? We didn't feel like praying. We said some words about my dad. My niece read out my mother's favourite prayer, which was the prayer she was going to read at the funeral later. My cousin's wife chatted away as we sat there afterwards, completely at ease. Graceful. Then my mother asked to be left alone with the coffin for a few minutes.

Outside, I admired the coat my cousin's wife was wearing. It was the only way I could communicate how grateful I felt towards her. The hearse driver and our driver and the second man in the hearse were all called Liam, they said. The three Liams were going to drive us to the crematorium via the canal, which is absolutely not the way to get to the crematorium from the hospital, in my opinion, but for once in my life I kept my mouth shut.

We made it in time, almost early. As the car swung in through the gates of the crematorium, I saw my friend and her husband leaving their car. This was the woman who had brought me enough food for four days and approved my new top on Sunday night. We'd been at school together; she'd known my father well. Why does she look so sad? I thought. And I saw her hair was wet. She always jumped into the shower at the last minute and ran out of the house with her hair wet. I remembered that from school assemblies, date nights, parties.

As we came up the drive, I began to see the faces of my friends who had gathered outside the church, not expecting to be amongst the chosen thirty-five who had seats inside for the ceremony. They applauded. Such a surprise. Something we had not had to organize ourselves.

The four grandchildren present took a corner of the coffin each and wheeled it up the aisle. My niece and my mother had picked the flowers that morning – it was a bit early for the daisies – and tied them with gardener's twine. I don't really remember going up the aisle behind the coffin. I remember that the chairs were all placed about four or five feet from each other, so that you would have to reach out to take someone's hand. The Lacrimosa was belting away. Our family felt very small. My sister was watching the funeral online with our Australian cousin in London. My brother was watching in Singapore with his wife and son.

The humanist celebrant, much subdued, introduced us. I welcomed everyone and read the Metta Sutta (edited version), and then the edited version of my nephew's poem. Then my nieces read their grandmother's favourite poem and a poem by Paul Durcan.

When choosing the music for his envisaged memorial service, my father, flagging a bit, had asked for 'something by Billy Joel'. Reader, I confess I couldn't find anything appropriate by Billy Joel, and substituted a song my father often sang, the Beatles' 'Blackbird', and actually it was better.

My cousin read out my Singapore brother's reflection on my father (slightly edited) and it was terrific. Then my brother delivered the eulogy. It touched on my father's medical work, his rugby, his golf, his politics.

And then, the moment I was dreading. The curtains – which

looked quite clean, in defiance of my mother's dire predictions —
began to close in front of the coffin. 'Mir ist so wunderbar'
was playing, but not loud enough. My mother wanted it
louder, but it wouldn't go any louder, we learned outside,
because of the format it had been saved on. I followed
my mother and my brother out, leaving my father's body
behind.

There was a lot of chatting and greeting outside, as those
who had been in the little crematorium met up with each
other and with those who had stood outside during the
ceremony. People had travelled from the country. My stepdaughter had crossed the city by DART and bus. There were
people I was surprised to see. Three of my Singapore
brother's friends had come to represent him. But we couldn't
shake hands, or hug. Quite a few of the older people were
wearing masks outside.

We went to my parents' local pub for a socially distanced
lunch. We sat at different tables. A friend of my father's gave
a very good speech, but it was cut short because we had
already outstayed the allotted time, and we had to leave.

My father couldn't take being teased, said his old friend as
we walked up the road to the house. He could dish it out,
but he couldn't take it. We were all under umbrellas now,
the old friend, my two nieces and myself. I can't take it
either, I said. My niece said that all her friends said the same
about her. My left foot felt funny. My sandal had broken.
And I was in the world of the bereaved, where what hurts is
not only how much has changed but also how little has
changed. The world where sandals break.

The next day, on my way to my friend's house for dinner, I was walking through the park and I watched a duck swimming with her ducklings. They don't know, I thought. They don't know that my father is dead.

Dermot Hourihane

1933–2020

Sources

This book is a work of journalism – a book about how we do death now, based on reporting done over the past five years. Its most important sources are the people who have spoken to me about their experiences and given me access to their lives and their expertise, and my biggest debt is to them. But death rituals have deep cultural roots – some deeper than others – and I have explored these as well. What follows is by no means a comprehensive listing of the literature on the culture of death in Ireland, but rather an acknowledgement of written sources (and an audio series) that I have drawn upon.

Adomnán of Iona, *Life of St Columba*, trans. Richard Sharpe (Penguin, 1995)

Beresford, David, *Ten Men Dead: The Story of the 1981 Hunger Strike* (Atlantic Monthly Press, 1997)

Bhreathnach, Edel, *Ireland in the Medieval World, AD 400–1000: Landscape, Kingship and Religion* (Four Courts Press, 2014)

Bitel, Lisa, 'Conceived in Sins, Born in Delights: Stories of Procreation from Early Ireland', *Journal of the History of Sexuality* (Vol. 3, No. 2, October 1992)

Bitel, Lisa, 'Sex, Sin and Celibacy in Early Christian Ireland', *Proceedings of the Harvard Celtic Colloquium* (Vol. 7, 1987, pp. 65–95)

Brown, Peter, *The Rise of Western Christendom: Triumph and Diversity, AD 200–1000* (Wiley-Blackwell, 1996 & 2003)

Carol, Anne, 'Embalming and the Materiality of Death (France, Nineteenth Century)', *Mortality* (Vol. 24, Issue 2, 2019)

Carson, Ciaran (trans.), *The Táin* (Penguin Classics, 2009)

Charles-Edwards, T. M., 'Érlam, the Patron Saint of an Irish Church', in *Local Saints and Local Churches in the Early Medieval West*, ed. Alan Thacker and Richard Sharpe (Oxford University Press, 2002)

Coakley, Davis, *Medicine in Trinity College Dublin: An Illustrated History* (Trinity College Dublin, 2014)

Connolly, Sean, 'Cogitosus's Life of St Brigit: Content and Value', *Journal of the Royal Society of Antiquaries of Ireland* (Vol. 117, 1987)

Connolly, Sean, 'Vita Prima Sanctae Brigitae: Background and Historical Value', *Journal of the Royal Society of Antiquaries of Ireland* (Vol. 119, 1989)

Craughwell, Thomas J., *Stealing Lincoln's Body* (Harvard University Press, 2004)

Deeny, James, *To Cure and to Care: Memoirs of a Chief Medical Officer* (Glendale Press, 1989)

Dennehy, Emer, 'Placeless Dead? Finding Evidence for Children in the Irish Landscape', *Journal of the History of Childhood and Youth* (Vol. 9, No. 2, Spring 2016)

Dennehy, Emer, and Lynch, Lydia, 'Unearthed Secrets: A Clandestine Burial Ground', *Archaeology Ireland* (Vol. 15, No. 4, 2001)

Dobson, Jessie, 'Some Eighteenth-Century Experiences of Embalming', *Journal of the History of Medicine and Allied Sciences* (Vol. 8, No. 4, October 1953)

Donnelly, Colm J., and Murphy, Eileen M., 'Children's Burial Grounds (Cillíní) in Ireland', in *Death and the Irish: A Miscellany*, ed. Salvador Ryan (Wordwell, 2016)

Farmer, David Hugh, *The Oxford Dictionary of Saints* (Oxford University Press, 1997)

Farrell, Brian, *Coroners: Practice and Procedure* (Round Hall Sweet & Maxwell, Dublin, 2000)

Flannery, Tony (ed.), *Responding to the Ryan Report* (Columba Press, 2009)

Fleetwood, John, 'The Dublin Body Snatchers, Part One', *Dublin Historical Record* (Vol. 42, No. 1, December 1988)

Fleetwood, John, 'The Dublin Body Snatchers, Part Two', *Dublin Historical Record* (Vol. 42, No. 2, March 1989)

Fleetwood, John, *The Irish Body Snatchers* (Tomar Publishing, 1988)

Kavanagh, Peter, *Beyond Affection: An Autobiography* (Peter Kavanagh Hand Press Incorporated, 1977)

Kavanagh, Peter, *Lapped Furrows: Correspondence 1933–1967* (Peter Kavanagh Hand Press Incorporated, 1969)

Kavanagh, Peter, *Patrick Kavanagh 1904–1967: A Life Chronicle* (Peter Kavanagh Hand Press Incorporated, 2000)

Kavanagh, Peter, *Sacred Keeper: A Biography of Patrick Kavanagh* (Goldsmith Press, 1979)

Keefe, Patrick Radden, *Say Nothing* (William Collins, 2018)

Keogh, Daire, 'Letterfrack: Peter Tyrell and the Ryan Report', in *Responding to the Ryan Report*, ed. Tony Flannery (Columba Press, 2009)

Largent-Christopher, Kimberly, 'Embalming Comes in Vogue During Civil War', *Washington Times* (2 April 2009)

Lee, Clive, *Surgeons' Halls: Building the Royal College of Surgeons in Ireland 1810–2010* (Royal College of Surgeons in association with A. & A. Farmar, 2011)

McKay, Susan, *Bear in Mind These Dead* (Faber & Faber, 2008)

McKee, Lyra, *In Her Own Words: Lost, Found, Remembered* (Faber & Faber, 2020)

McKittrick, David, et al., *Lost Lives: The Stories of the Men, Women and Children who Died as a Result of the Northern Ireland Troubles* (Mainstream Publishing Company, 1999)

McLaughlin, Mary, 'Keening the Dead: Ancient History or a Ritual for Today?', *Religions* (Vol. 10, No. 4, 2019)

Milligan, Becky (producer), *The Home Babies*, 11 episodes, BBC Radio Four

Milotte, Mike, *Banished Babies: The Secret History of Ireland's Baby Export Business* (2nd edn, New Island, 2012)

Moloney, Ed, *A Secret History of the IRA* (Penguin, 2002)

Moore, Wendy, *The Knife Man: Blood, Body-Snatching and the Birth of Modern Surgery* (Bantam, 2005)

Morris, Henry, 'Irish Wake Games', *Béaloideas* (Iml. VIII, Uimh 2, December 1938)

Mytum, Harold, 'Combating Dublin Body-Snatchers: The Drumcondra Mortsafe', *Archaeology Ireland* (Vol. 27, No. 4, Winter 2013)

Nic Suibhne, Fionnuala, '"On the Straw" and Other Aspects of Pregnancy and Childbirth from the Oral Tradition of the Women in Ulster', *Ulster Folklife* (Vol. 38, 1992)

O'Brien, Elizabeth, 'Into the west: a fifth/sixth century lady and her horse join the ancestors', in *Death and the Irish: a Miscellany*, ed. Salvador Ryan (Wordwell, 2016)

Ó Cadhain, Máirtín, *Graveyard Clay / Cré na Cille*, trans. Liam Mac Con Iomaire and Tim Robinson (Yale University Press, 2016)

O'Connor, Anne, *The Blessed and the Damned: Sinful Women and Unbaptised Children in Irish Folklore* (Peter Lang, 2005)

Ó Crualaoich, Gearóid, 'The "Merry Wake"', in *Irish Popular Culture 1650–1850*, ed. J. S. Donnelly Jr and Kerby A. Miller (Irish Academic Press, 1998)

Ó Súilleabháin, Seán, 'Adhlacadh Leanbhaí', *Journal of the Royal Society of Antiquaries of Ireland* (Vol. 9, No. 3, September 1939) (translated for me by Tony O'Flatharta)

Ó Súilleabháin, Seán, *Irish Wake Amusements* (Mercier Press, 1967)

O'Sullivan, Eoin, and O'Donnell, Ian, *Coercive Confinement in Ireland: Patients, prisoners and penitents* (Manchester University Press, 2012)

Raftery, Mary, and O'Sullivan, Eoin, *Suffer the Little Children: The Inside Story of Ireland's Industrial Schools* (New Island, 1999)

Ryan, Salvador, *Death and the Irish: A Miscellany* (Wordwell, 2016)

Scraton, Phil, and McNaull, Gillian, 'Death Investigation, Coroners' Inquests and the Rights of the Bereaved', Irish Council for Civil Liberties (April 2021)

Sehgal, Parul, '"Eat The Buddha" Reports from the "World Capital of Self-Immolations"', *New York Times* (15 July 2020)

Troyer, John, *Technologies of the Human Corpse* (MIT Press, 2020)

Tuairim, London Branch Study Group, 'Some of Our Children: a report on residential care of the deprived' (Tuairim, 1966)

Tyrrell, Peter, *Founded on Fear, Letterfrack Industrial School, War and Exile*, ed. and with an introduction by Diarmuid Whelan (Irish Academic Press, 2006)

Underwood, Emily, 'Landscape of Dead Bodies May Have Inspired First Mummies', *Science* (13 August 2012)

Verini, James, 'A Terrible Act of Reason: When Did Self-Immolation Become the Paramount Form of Protest?', *New Yorker* (16 May 2012)

Williams, Paul, *Mahayana Buddhism: The Doctrinal Foundations* (2nd edn, Routledge, 2009)

Wood-Martin, W. G., *Traces of the Elder Faiths of Ireland: A Folklore Sketch, Volume 1* (Longmans, Green & Co., 1902)

Acknowledgements

In writing this book, I have relied greatly on the goodwill and the openness of many different people and institutions. I have been extraordinarily fortunate in the number and variety of people, all over Ireland, who were kind enough to allow me to hear their stories – frequently very hard stories of great suffering. They let me into their lives and places of work, gave me their time and trusted me with their experiences. Their generosity forms the bedrock of this book, and I am grateful to them all.

For granting me the access that made it possible for me to speak to Bernie Brady Walsh and other people at the end of their lives, I am especially grateful to Our Lady's Hospice at Harold's Cross in Dublin. Jeanne McDonagh, then public relations executive there, immediately understood the purpose of the book and smoothed my path; and the medical team there allowed me to follow their work and responded tirelessly to my questions. I want also to thank the patients at the hospice, whose kindness and good humour towards a stranger made my work there in many ways a pleasure.

My family and friends provided support, encouragement, and sometimes rather robust advice, for which I now find myself surprisingly grateful. The staff at Dublin City Libraries and at the Berkeley Library at Trinity College, where

I worked so happily before the pandemic hit, also have my gratitude. I have been lucky with both my agent, Jonathan Williams, and my publisher. I want to thank Michael McLoughlin at Sandycove for his enthusiasm and encouragement, as well as Jane Selley, my copy-editor, and editorial assistant Isabelle Hanrahan, for all they did to bring this book to completion. Finally, thanks to Brendan Barrington, my editor, for his work ethic, his high standards, and his kindness during the writing of this book, when we both encountered death within our respective families.